Charles Hindley

The History of the Catnach Press

Charles Hindley

The History of the Catnach Press

ISBN/EAN: 9783744731850

Printed in Europe, USA, Canada, Australia, Japan

Cover: Foto ©ninafisch / pixelio.de

More available books at **www.hansebooks.com**

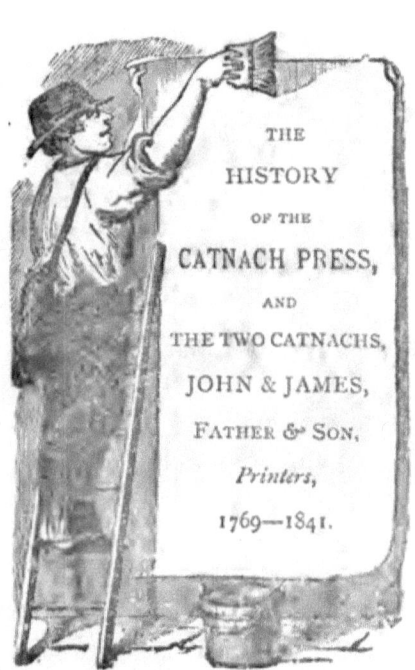

THE HISTORY OF THE CATNACH PRESS.

———:)o(:———

LARGE PAPER COPY.

Only Two Hundred and Fifty Printed. Each Copy numbered and Signed

No. 67

Purchased by

_____

of

_____

on the _____ *day of* _____ 18___

THE
HISTORY
OF THE
CATNACH PRESS,

AT
BERWICK-UPON-TWEED,
ALNWICK AND NEWCASTLE-UPON-TYNE,
IN NORTHUMBERLAND,
AND
SEVEN DIALS, LONDON.

BY

CHARLES HINDLEY, Esq.,

Editor of "The Old Book Collector's Miscellany; or, a Collection of Readable Reprints of Literary Rarities," "Works of John Taylor—the Water Poet," "The Roxburghe Ballads," "The Catnach Press," "The Curiosities of Street Literature," The Book of Ready Made Speeches," "Life and Times of James Catnach, late of the Seven Dials, Ballad Monger," "Tavern Anecdotes and Sayings," "A History of the Cries of London—Ancient and Modern," etc.

𝕷𝖔𝖓𝖉𝖔𝖓:
CHARLES HINDLEY
[THE YOUNGER,]
BOOKSELLERS' ROW, ST. CLEMENT DANES,
STRAND, W.C.

1886.

TO

Mr. GEORGE SKELLY,

OF

THE MARKET PLACE,

AND

Mr. GEORGE H. THOMPSON,

OF

BAILIFFGATE, ALNWICK,

In the County of

NORTHUMBERLAND,

THE

HISTORY OF THE CATNACH PRESS,

IS MOST RESPECTFULLY DEDICATED BY

THE AUTHOR

Charles Hindley

St. James' Street, Brighton.
Lady Day, 1886.

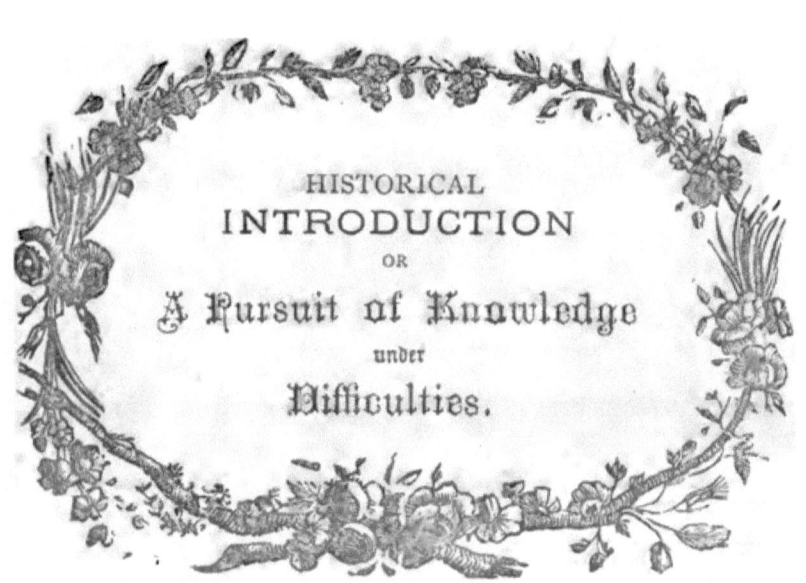

HISTORICAL
INTRODUCTION
OR
A Pursuit of Knowledge
under
Difficulties.

THE CATNACH PRESS.

" 'Tis education forms the common mind ;
Just as the twig is bent the tree's inclined."—*Pope.*

——————There can be little doubt that Jemmy Catnach, the printer, justly earned the distinction of being one of the great pioneers in the cause of promoting cheap literature—he was for a long time the great Mæcenas and Elzevir of the Seven Dials district. We do not pretend to say that the productions which emanated from his establishment contained much that was likely to enlighten the intellect, or sharpen the taste of the ordinary reader ; but, to a great extent, they served well in creating an impetus in the minds of many to soar after things of a higher and more ennobling character. Whilst for the little folk his store was like the conjuror's bag—inexhaustible. He could cater to the taste and fancies of all, and it is marvellous, even in these days of a cheap press, to look back upon the time when this enterprising man was by a steady course of action, so paving the way for that bright day in the annals of Britain's history, when every child in the land should be educated.

HISTORICAL INTRODUCTION

OR

A PURSUIT OF KNOWLEDGE UNDER DIFFICULTIES.

———KNOWLEDGE is of two kinds. We know a subject ourselves, or we know where we can find information upon it.—BOSWELL, *Life of Johnson.*

THAT history repeats itself is fairly and fully exemplified by the reproduction of " THE CATNACH PRESS," the *first* edition of which was published in 1869, and " GUARANTEED ONLY TWO HUNDRED AND FIFTY COPIES PRINTED."—Namely: 175 on fine, and 75 on extra thick paper. *Each copy numbered.* The outer and descriptive title set forth that the work contained :—

"A COLLECTION of Books and Wood-cuts of James Catnach, late of Seven Dials, Printer, consisting of Twenty Books of the Cock Robin-Class, from, 'This is the House that Jack Built,' to 'Old Mother Hubbard,'(printed with great care) *specialite* at THE CATNACH PRESS, from the old plates and woodcuts, prior to their final destruction, to which is added a selection of Catnachian wood-cuts, many by Bewick, and many of the most anti-Bewickian character it is possible to conceive."

The announcement of the publication of the work was first made known through the medium of the metropolitan press, some few days prior to the copies being delivered by the bookbinders, and so great was the demand of the London and American trade, that every copy was disposed of on the day of issue.

The work is now eagerly sought after by book collectors who indulge in literary rarities.

While engaged in collecting information for "The Catnach Press," and interviewing the producers of ballads, broadsides and chap-books, we met with a vast assemblage of street-papers and of a very varied character, which we proposed to publish in quarto form under the title of "The Curiosities of Street Literature," and when in London in 1869, still seeking for information on the subject, met by mere chance in the Strand with the street ballad singer of our youth, one Samuel Milnes, who used between the years of 1835 and 1842 to visit Fetter Lane every Thursday with the newest and most popular ballad of the day. We so often met with him at other times and places in and about London in after years that a peculiar kind of a friendly feeling grew up towards him in preference to all other street ballad singers of the time, so much so that at our meetings—and friendly greetings, we invariably purchased the ballad he was singing, or, gave him a few halfpence as a fee for having detained him from his calling—or shall we say bawling, for to tell the truth, Samuel Milnes was but a very indifferent vocalist.

Time rolled on—"still on it creeps, each little moment at another's heels"—and we continued to meet our old ballad singer either in London or Brighton. The meeting with him on this particular occasion was most opportune for we wanted him. First we obtained from him "Wait for the Turn of the Tide," and "Call her back and kiss her," then the following information :—

"Oh, yes, I remember you, remember you well; particularly when I see you down at Brighton; when you treated me to that hot rum and water;

when I was so wet and cold, **at a** little snug public-house in **one** of the streets that leads off the **main** street. I don't remember the name **on** it now, but I remembers the rum and water well enough; it was good. You said it would be, and so it **was, and no mistake.** How old am I **now?** Why, 59. How long have I been at it? Why, hard on fifty years. **I** was about nine or ten year old—no, perhaps I might have been 12 year old, when I come to think on it. **Yes,** about 12 year old; my mother **was a** widow with five children, and there was a boy in our street as used **to** go out singing ballads, and his mother said to my mother, 'Why don't you let your boy (that's me) go out and sing ballads like my boy.' And I said I didn't mind, and I did go out, and I've been at it ever since, so you see 'aint far short of 50 year. How many do I sell in a day? Well, not so many as I used to do, by a long way. I've sold me four and five quires a-day, but I don't sell above two and three dozen a-day now. That's all the difference you see, sir—dozens against quires. How do I live then? Why, you see I am so well-known in different parts of London, that lots and lots of people comes up to me like you always do—and say's—'How do you do, old fellow? I remember you when I was a boy, if it's a man, and when I was a girl, if it's a woman.' And says, 'So you are still selling songs, eh?' Then they give me a few coppers; some more and some less than others, and says they don't want the songs. Some days—very often—I've had more money given me than I've took for the ballads. Yes, I have travelled all over England—all over it I think—but the North's the best—Manchester, Liverpool, and them towns; but down Bath and Cheltenham way I was nearly starved. I was coming back from that way, I now remember, when I met you, sir, at Brighton that time. I buy my ballads at various places—but now mostly over the water, because I live there now and it's handiest. Mr. Such, the printer, in Union-street in the Borough. Oh! yes, some at Catnach's—leastways, it ain't Catnach's now, it's Fortey's. Yes, I remember 'old Jemmy Catnach' very well; he wa'n't a bad sort, as you say; leastways, I've heard so, but I never had anything of him. I always paid for what I had, and did not say much to him, or he to me—Writing the life of him, are you indeed? No, I can't give you no more information about him than that, because, as I said before, I bought my goods as I wanted them, and paid for them, then away on my own account and business. Well he was a man something **like** you—a little wider across the shoulders, perhaps, but about such a man as you are. **I did** know a man as could have told you a lot **about** "old Jemmy," **but he's** dead now; he was one of his authors, that is, he wrote **some of the** street-ballads for him, and very good ones they used to be, that is, for selling. Want some old 'Dying Speeches' and 'Cocks,' do you indeed; well, I a'nt got any—I don't often 'work' them things, although I have done so sometimes, but I mostly keep to the old game—' Ballads on a Subject.' You see them other things are no use only just for the day, then they are no use at all, so we don't keep them—I've often given them away. You'd give sixpence a piece for them, would you, indeed, sir; then I wish I had some of them. Now I come to think of it I know a man that did have a lot of them bye him, and I know he'd be glad to sell them, I don't know where he lives, but I sometimes see him. Oh! yes, a letter would find me. My name is Samuel Milnes, and I live at No. 81, Mint-street, that's in the Borough; you know, Guagar is the name at the house. Thank you, sir, I'm much obliged. Good day sir."

Our next adventure—in pursuit of knowledge under difficulties—occured at Brighton in the month of August, 1869, and when we were winding our way through a maze of small streets lying between Richmond and Albion Hills, in the Northern part of the town, our ears voluntarily "pricked up," on hearing the old familiar sounds of a 'street, or running patterer' with the stereotyped sentences of "Horrible."—"Dreadful."—"Remarkable letters found on his person."—"Cut down by a labouring man."—Quite dead."—"Well-known in the town."—"Hanging." —"Coroner's Inquest."—"Verdict."—"Full particulars."— "Most determined suicide."—"Brutal conduct."—&c., &c., *Only a ha'penny!—Only a ha'penny!* Presently we saw the man turn into a wide court-like place, which was designated by the high-sounded name of "SQUARE," and dedicted to RICHMOND; hither we followed him, and heard him repeat the same detached sentences, and became a purchaser for—'*only a ha'penny!*' when to our astonishment we discovered a somewhat new phrase in cock or catchpenny selling. Inasmuch as our purchase consisted of the current number (253) of the *Brighton Daily News*—a very respectable looking and well printed Halfpenny Local Newspaper, and of that day's publication, and did in reality contain an account of a most determined suicide of an old and highly respected inhabitant of Brighton and set forth under the heading of :—

THE DETERMINED SUICIDE OF AN AGED ARTIST.
REMARKABLE LETTERS OF DECEASED.

Calling the man aside, we ventured upon a conversation with him in the following form :—

——"Well, governor, *how does the cock fight?*" "Oh, pretty well, sir; but it ain't a cock; its a genuine thing—the days for cocks, sir, is gone bye—cheap newspapers 'as done 'em up." "Yes; we see this is a Brighton Newspaper of to-day." "Oh, yes, that's right enough—but its all true." "Yes; we are aware of that and knew the unfortunate man and his family; but you are vending them after the old manner." That's all right enough, sir,—you see I can sell 'em better in that form than as a newspaper—its more natural like for me: I've sold between ten and twelve dozen of 'em to-day." "Yes; but how about to-morrow?." "Oh, then it will be all bottled up—and I must look for a new game, I'm on my way to London, but a hearing of this suicide job, I thought I'd work 'em just to keep my hand in and make a bob or two." To our question of " Have you got any real old 'cocks' by you?" He replied, "No, not a bit of a one; I've worked 'em for a good many years, but it 'aint much of a go now. Oh, yes, I know'd 'old Jemmy Catnach' fast enough—bought many hundreds, if not thousands of quires of him. Not old enough? Oh, 'aint I though; why I'm turned fifty, and I've been a 'street-paper' seller all my life. I knows Muster Fortey very well; him as is got the business now in the Dials—he knows his way about, let him alone for that; and he's a rare good business man let me tell you, and always been good and fair to me; that I will say of him."

Having rewarded the man with a few half-pence to make him some recompense for having detained him during his business progress, we parted company.

While still prosecuting our enquiries for information on the literature of the streets, we often read of, and heard mention made of, a Mr. John Morgan, as one of the "Seven Bards of the

Seven Dials" and his being best able to assist us in the matter we had in hand. The first glimpse we obtained of the Poet! in print was in an article entitled "The Bards of the Seven Dials and their Effusion" and published in "THE TOWN," of 1839, a weekly journal, conducted by the late Mr. Renton Nicholson, better known as "Baron Nicholson," of Judge and Jury notoriety :—

REVIEW.

*The Life and Death of John **William Marchant**,* who suffered the extreme penalty of the law, **in front of the Debtor's door, Newgate,** on Monday, July 8th, 1839, for the murder of Elizabeth Paynton, his fellow servant, on the seventeenth of May last, in Cadogan Place, Chelsea. By John Morgan. London: J. Catnach, 2 and 3, Monmouth Court, 7 Dials.

The work is a quarto page, surrounded with a handsome black border. "Take no thought for to-morrow, what thou shalt eat, or what thou shalt put on," says a certain writer, whose wisdom we all reverence, and then he adds " Sufficient unto the day is the evil thereof"—a remark particularly applicable to the bards of Seven Dials, whose pens are kept in constant employment by the fires, rapes, robberies, and murders, which, from one year's end to the other, present them with a daily allowance of evil sufficient for their subsistence. But, at present, it is only one of these poets, "John Morgan," as he modestly signs himself, whom we are about to notice; and as some of our readers may be curious to see a specimen of the poetry of Seven Dials, we shall lay certain portions of John Morgan's last effusion before them, pointing out the beauties and peculiarities of the compositions as we go along. After almost lawyer-like particularity as to dates and places, the poem begins with an invocation from the murderer in *propria personæ*.

> "Oh! give attention awhile to me,
> All you good people of each degree;
> In Newgate's dismal and dreary cell,
> I bid all people on earth farewell."

Heaven forbid, say we, that *all* the people on earth should ever get in Newgate, to receive the farewell of such a blood-thirsty miscreant.

xiii.

> "John William Marchant is my name,
> I do confess I have *been to blame*."

And here we must observe that the poet makes his hero speak of his offence rather too lightly, as if, indeed, it had been nothing more than a common misdemeanour.

> "I little thought, my dear parents kind,
> I should leave this earth with a troubled mind."

Now this *is* modest; he is actually surprised that his parents are at all grieved at the idea of getting rid of such a scoundrel, and well he might be.

> "I lived as servant in Cadogan Place,
> And never thought this would be my case,
> To end my days on the fatal tree:
> Good people, pray drop a tear for me."

There is a playfulness **about the word** "drop," introducing just here after "the fatal tree," which, in our mind, somewhat diminishes the plaintiveness of the entreaty; but **we must not be hypocritical.**

* * * * * * * * *
* * * * * * * * *

Then comes his trial and condemnation, **the account of which is most** remarkable precise and pithy.

> "At the Old Bailey I was tried and cast,
> And the dreadful sentence on me was past
> On a Monday morning, alas! to die,
> And on the eight of this month of July."

A marvellous particularity as to dates, intended, doubtless, **to show the** convicts anxiety that, although he died young, his name should live long in the minds of posterity. Then follows his farewell to father and mother, and an impudent expression of confidence that his crime will be forgiven in heaven, an idea, by-the-by, **which is reported to** have been confirmed by the Ordinary of Newgate, who told him that the angels would receive him with great affection; and this it was, perhaps, which induced our bard of Seven Dials to represent his hero as coolly writing poetry up to the very last moment of his existence; taking his farewell of the public in these words:—

> "Adieu, good people of each degree,
> And take a warning, I pray, by me;
> The bell is tolling, and I must go,
> And leave this world of misery and woe."

But we cannot exactly see what business the fellow—"a pampered menial," had to speak ill of the world, when he was very comfortably off in it, and might have lived long and happily if it had not been for his own wickedness; a hint which we throw out for the benefit of Mr. John Morgan, in his future effusions, trusting he will not make his heroes die grumby, when poetic justices does not require it.

But we must now take our leave, with a hearty wish to the whole fraternity of Seven Dials' bards, that they may never go without a dinner for want of the means of earning it, or that, in other words, though they seem somewhat contradictory, "Sufficient unto the day may be the evil thereof."

Again, the writer of an article on "Street Ballads," in the "National Review," for October, 1861, makes the following remarks:—

"This Ballad—'Little Lord John out of Service'—is one of the few which bear a signature—it is signed 'John Morgan' in the copy which we possess. For a long time we believed this name to be a mere *nom-de-plume*, but the other day in Monmouth Court, we were informed, in answer to a casual question that this is the real name of the author of some of the best comic ballads. Our informant added that he is an elderly, we may say old, gentleman, living somewhere in Westminster; but the exact whereabouts we could not discover. Mr. Morgan followed no particular visible calling, so far as our informant knew, except writing ballads, by which he could not earn much of a livelihood, as the price of an original ballad, in these buying-cheap days, has been screwed down by the publishers to somewhere about a shilling sterling. Something more like bread-and-butter might be made, perhaps, by poets who were in the habit of singing their own ballads, as some of them do, but not Mr. Morgan. Should this ever meet the eye of that gentleman (a not very probable event, we fear), we beg to apologise for the liberty we have taken in using his verses and name, and hope he will excuse us, having regard to the subject in which we are humble fellow-labourers. We could scarcely avoid naming him, the fact being that he is the only living author of street-ballads whose name we know. That self-denying mind, indifferent to worldly fame, which characterised the architects of our cathedrals and abbeys, would seem to have descended on our ballad-writers; and we must be thankful, therefore, to be able to embalm and hand down to posterity a name here and there, such as William of Wykeham, and John Morgan. In answer to our inquiries in this matter, generally, we have been told, 'Oh, anybody writes them,' and with that answer we have had to rest satisfied. But in presence of that answer, we walk about the streets with a new sense of wonder, peering into the faces of those of our fellow-lieges who do not carry about with them **the external evidence of overflowing exchequers, and saying to ourselves That man may be a writer of ballads.'"**

At every enquiry we made for information in regard to street-literature, we still continued to be referred to Mr. John Morgan as the most likely person living to supply what we needed on the subject.

But the grave question arose in our own minds of the How, When, and Where: could we find out and interview this said Mr. John Morgan, Poet! First we made enquiry at the office of Mr. Taylor, Printer of Ballads, &c., 92 and 93, Brick Lane, Spitalfields, but, they "had not the least idea where we could find him. In fact they had only heard of him as a ballad-writer, and knew nothing about where he lived, never having employed him: had perhaps printed some of his ballads. Thought Mr. Such, of the Borough, might give some information, but, sure to find out all about him in the Seven Dials district."

Mr. H. Such, Machine Printer and Publisher, 177, Union Street, Borough, S.E., on being applied to could give us no positive information as to the whereabout of Mr. John Morgan —he knew him, but where he lived he could not tell. Mr. Fortey or Mr. Disley, in the Dials-way, would be most likely to know.

Mr. William S. Fortey, (late A. Ryle, successor to the late J. Catnach), Printer, Publisher, and Wholesale Stationer, 2 and 3, Monmouth Court, Seven Dials, London, W., on being applied to could not exactly tell where Mr. John Morgan did live, it was somewhere Westminster-way: it was very uncertain when he should next see him, because he did not sometimes call in for weeks together, yet he might by chance see him to-morrow, or the next day. Anyway, we felt that we had no right to press the question any further, more particularly so because Mr. Fortey had been very civil and obliging to us on other occasions—in fact we have been under great and lasting obligations to him, so changed the conversation.

Mr. Henry Disley, Printer, 57, High Street, St. Giles', London, who we found to be a very genial sort of a man, and that he had formerly been in the service of James Catnach; he was working in his front shop at a small hand-press on some cards relative to a forthcoming FRIENDLY LEAD,* to be held at a public-house in the immediate neighbourhood, while Mrs. Disley was hard at work colouring some Christmas Carols, and which she did with a rapidity that was somewhat astonishing. In answer to our inquiry whether he knew of one John Morgan—who was—as we described him, "something of a song writer." Well! both Mr. and Mrs. Disley together—"did know him—should think they did." But when we came to enquire about his private address they knew nothing about that. He (Mr. Morgan) wrote ballads for them at times: often called on them—whenever he did it was always to sell a *good* ballad he had on hand, or to tell them what *bad* times it-was with him: but as to where he lived, beyond that it was somewhere Westminster-way, they did not know—in fact, had not the least idea. But, most likely, Mr. Fortey, him in Monmouth Court, did. Yes! come to think of it, he would be sure to know.

---

* FRIENDLY LEAD, a gathering at a low public-house, for the purpose of assisting some one who is "in trouble," *i.e.*, in prison, or who has just "come out of trouble," or who is in want of a "mouthpiece" to defend him, and so forth.

The very unsatisfactory and evasive answers received in reference to the address of Mr. John Morgan gave a zest to our zeal in the matter—so much so, that we then determined "to work the oracle" out in our way.

At this time we had a near relative occupying chambers in Barnard's Inn, which we held to be a good central and lawyer-like address—one that had the "true ring," of business and substantiality about it. Yes! Barnard's Inn, Holborn, London, E.C., looked to our mind to be likely to serve our stratigical purpose to the point we desired. Having made all the preparatory arrangements, we then procured from a neighbouring stationer's shop a sheet of mourning note-paper and an envelope of large proportions, each having the very blackest and broadest of black borders we could find in stock. Then we wrote in a law-like hand :—

No. 6, Barnard's Inn,
Holborn, London, E.C.,
February 26, 1870.

THIS IS TO GIVE NOTICE:—If Mr. John Morgan, ballad-writer, &c., will call at the above address on or after Wednesday next. He will hear something greatly to his advantage.

(Signed)

Charles Hindley

Mr. John Morgan,
    care of..................................
        ....*London.*

The above document having been duly intrusted to Her Majesty's Post Master General for delivery, we had to abide our time for the result. We had not to wait long, for although we had appointed the next following Wednesday to communicate "*something greatly to the advantage of Mr. John Morgan,*" he turned up a little sooner than we expected, or desired, by reason of his putting in an appearance at Barnard's Inn on Tuesday evening, where he arrived "happy and glorious," and made earnest enquiries for "the gentleman who had sent him a letter to say he had got a something to his advantage—perhaps a fortune ! For sometimes he thought somebody would die and leave him one. Where was the gentleman who wrote him the letter? He says that I am to call here. He sent it in a black-bordered envelope for him. Where is the gentleman? See here is the letter, and all in black—black as your hat—look for yourself, sir."

All the above was spoken to a friend of ours who lived on the ground-floor at the particular house in Barnard's Inn, where Mr. John Morgan had been requested to call on Wednesday. It was then only Tuesday, and that fact had to be explained; also, that the gentleman in question was not at present in his chambers on the third-floor, but would be in the morning up to 10 o'clock. Our friend on the first-floor—who had received instructions from us in the event of Mr. John Morgan turning-up while we were not at home—informed us of all that had taken place when we arrived a little later on in the evening.

On the next morning preparations were made for the reception of our expectant friend—a good fire, a good breakfast, and a half-pint of "Old Tom" from Carr's well-known Establishment, St. Clement Danes, Strand.

Very soon after the old clock of the ancient hall of Barnard's Inn, and all the public clocks in the surrounding neighbourhood had proclaimed aloud that the hour of 10 a.m. of that Wednesday morning had arrived, there was heard a knock at the outer door of our chamber-rooms, and on the same being opened, Mr. John Morgan announced himself as the party to whom the gentleman had sent a black-bordered letter and envelope for him to say there was a something to his advantage to be had. Then Mr. John Morgan, full of bows and scrapes, was ushered into our presence.—He was the party who had received the letter. Oh! yes, Mr. Morgan we added: take a seat sir. Yes, sir, and thank you to, he replied, at the same time sitting down and then very carefully despositing his somewhat delapidated hat under—far under—the chair. We then enquired whether he would have anything to eat, or have a cup of coffee. No! it was a little too early in the morning for eating, and coffee did not always agree with him. Or, a drop of good "Old Tom," we somewhat significantly suggested. Mr. John Morgan would very much like to have a little drop of gin, for it was a nasty raw cold morning: In answer to our enquiry whether he would prefer hot or cold water, elected to have it neat if it made no difference to us.

Mr. John Morgan at our suggestion having "wet the other eye," *i.e.*, taken the second glass, the real business part of the question we had met upon commenced thus:—"We have been informed that you were acquainted with, and used to write for the late James Catnach, who formerly lived in the Seven Dials, and that you can give us much of the information that we require towards perfecting a work we have in hand treating on Street Literature. If you are willing to do so, we are prepared to treat with you in a liberal manner, and that, please to at once to understand is the '*Something greatly to your advantage* that is mentioned in the note we addressed to you.'" Here Mr. John Morgan hinted that he thought it was—or he had hoped it was, a little fortune some one had been kind enough to leave him, he always expected that old Jemmy Catnach would—after what he had done for him, have left him a bit, however small, but no such luck.

Mr. Morgan expressed his willingness to give all the information he could on the subject and leave it to our generosity to pay him what we pleased, and adding that he had no doubt that we should not fall out on that score. And so we proceeded, we talked and took notes. Mr. Morgan talked and took gin. Mr. Morgan got warm—warmer and warmer—and very entertaining, his conversational powers increased wonderfully, he became very witty and laughed *ha*! *hah*!! he joked and made merry at some old reminiscences in connection with old Jemmy Catnach—and admitted, that after all old Jemmy wasn't a particular bad sort— that is, when you knew him, and could handle him properly— then old Jemmy was as right as my leg! Still we continued to talk and take notes, still Mr. Morgan talked and took gin, until he emulated the little old woman who sold "Hot Codlings," for of her it is related that—" the glass she filled and the bottle she shrunk and that this little old woman in the end got——."

At length it became very manifest that we should not be able to get any more information out of Mr. John Morgan on that day, so proposed for him to call again on the morrow morning and at the same time and place to pursue the thread of our narrative. Then having presented him with a portrait of Her most gracious Majesty Queen Victoria, set in gold, we volunteered to see him down stairs which we observed were very crooked—Mr. Morgan thought they were very old and funny ones: up and down like—in fact what old Charley Dibdin would have called regular " whopping old stairs!" Being safely landed from the last stone step on to the stone-paved way, we thought it advisable, for appearance sake, to conduct our friend out of Barnard's

Inn by a sideway leading into Fetter-lane. After that it occurred to us that it would perhaps be better to see him to the Fleet-street end of the lane and then to put him into a Westminster omnibus, but we had reached Somerset House before one going that way came in sight. Then it was Mr. John Morgan suddenly recollected that he could not pass his old friend Short—who was Short? why surely you know Short—old Short, him as sells the wine so good and so cheap, there over the way—that's Short's—"WINES FROM THE WOOD," that's out of the cask you know, you remind me to-morrow, sir, and I'll tell you a good tale about old Short before he made such a lot of money as he has got now.—Capital chap old Short, he knows me—it's all about a song I wrote—but I'll tell you all about it to-morrow. Besides I must have change ye know for there's no one got any at my home—my landlord—There's no change about him, Oh! dear no—He's never got any change but he's always got an old account, do you see? an old account—but no matter let's go in!

Respectfully, but firmly declining the kind and very pressing invitation to have "only just one drop with old Short." We left Mr. John Morgan to take care of himself for the day and to be sure to meet us on the next morning in Barnard's Inn at 10 o'clock—sharp.

At length the wishful morrow came, also ten of the clock, but not so Mr. John Morgan, nor did he call at any hour during the day. But soon after 11 o'clock the next day he made his appearance, but being so stupidly drunk we gave him some money and told him to call again to-morrow. And he did, but still so muddled that we could make nothing out of him, so we somewhat curtly dismissed him and returned to Brighton.

The next day the letter—of which we give a *verbatim et literatim* copy—was received and then forwarded on to us.

xxii.

90 Great Peter Street
Westminister, S.W.

Saturday the 5th of March 1870.

My Dear and Kind Sir :—I return you my most sincere and heartfelt thanks for the Kindness I received from you and deeply I regret if I caused you any displeasure the fact is I have been greatly put about And you having been so kind as to give me refreshments it overpowered me I fell and hurt myself. And I am now destitute without a penny in the world or a friend to help me. I feel as though I offended you I hope not I think by the Little conversation we had I may be able to please you I have been considering in my doleful moments matters of importance if my kind and good friend you can favour me with a Line this Saturday Evening I will be most grateful I shall not go out waiting to hear from you I am placed in a most Sad position accept my thanks write Me a Line in answer to this Befriend me if it is possible And I will make all right and with gratitude.

Anxiously waiting your kind and I trust favourable reply,

Your Humble Servt
John Morgan

Charles Hindley, Esq
6 Barnard's Inn
Holborn
W.C.

Having no desire to incur the expense of another journey to London in the matter, and believing that we had obtained sufficient information on the subject, we published, in the year 1871, a limited number of copies of our work under the title of :—

CURIOSITIES
OF
STREET LITERATURE:
COMPRISING
"COCKS," OR "CATCHPENNIES,"

A Large and Curious Assortment of

STREET DROLLERIES, SQUIBS, HISTORIES, COMIC STORIES
IN PROSE AND VERSE,

BROADSIDES ON THE ROYAL FAMILY,

POLITICAL LITANIES, DIALOGUES, CATECHISMS, ACTS OF PARLIAMENT,
STREET POLITICAL PAPERS.

A VARIETY OF "BALLADS ON A SUBJECT,"

DYING SPEECHES AND CONFESSIONS,

TO WHICH IS ATTACHED THE ALL-IMPORTANT AND NECESSARY

AFFECTIONATE COPY OF VERSES,
AS

"Come, all you feeling-hearted Christians, wherever you may be,
Attention give to these few lines, and listen unto me;
It's of this cruel murder, to you I will unfold,
The bare recital of the same will make your blood run cold."

—:o:—

"What hast here? ballads? I love a ballad in print, or a life; for then we are sure they are true."—*Shakespeare.*

"There's nothing beats a stunning good murder, after all."—*Experiences of a Running Patterer.*

—:o:—

LONDON:
REEVES AND TURNER
196, STRAND,

1871.

CURIOSITIES OF STREET LITERATURE.

Guaranteed only Four Hundred and Fifty Six Copies Printed,

NAMELY,—

			£	s.	d.
250	on Fine Toned Demy 4to ... ... Published at	1	1	0
100	on Large Post 4to, printed on one side of the paper only ...	,,	1	5	0
100	on Fine French Linear Writing Paper, printed on one side only, and in imitation of the Catnachian tea-like paper of old ...	,,	1	11	6
6	on Yellow Demy 4to paper	,,	2	2	0

456

☞ **EACH COPY OF EACH EDITION NUMBERED.**

XXV.

Our work on the Curiosities of Street Literature soon ran out of print. But we continued to gather from time to time fresh information on the subject of the "Two Catnachs—John and James," and in the early part of 1876 we determined on publishing a work, to be entitled "The Life and Times of James Catnach—late of Seven Dials—Ballad Monger." And for the purpose of obtaining the verification, amendment, or denial to the several scraps of information we had obtained, we wrote to our old friend, Mr. John Morgan, on the subject, and from him we received the letters that follow :—

> No. 1, Model Cottages, Little St. Anne's Lane,
> Great Peter Street, Westminster,
> London, S.W.
> *16th February,* 1876.
>
> Sir,
>
> I received your Letter this Morning: I have removed to above address two years and seven months, I have been in Bed seven weeks suffering from Bronchitis; but am now recovering and shall get up to-day, but the Doctor will not permit me to go out.
>
> Whatever you may require I am ready and willing to do to the utmost of my abilities, and be happy to serve you, and much regret I have not the strength to venture to————Street. If anything can be done by Letter or otherwise, I will willingly attend to your request, your reply will greatly oblige,
>
> *Your Humble Servt.*
>
> *John Morgan.*
>
> P.S.—Please excuse the illegible scribble as I write this in Bed.

Charles Hindley, Esq.,
  76, Rose Hill Terrace, Brighton.

xxvi.

No. 1, Model Cottages, Little St. Ann's Lane,
Great Peter Street, Westminster, London, S.W.
17th February, 1876.

Sir,
I have just received yours, 7 p.m., and in reply I beg to say that when I came to London in 1818 Catnach's Father was not living.

Catnach, his Mother, and Sister Julia the youngest, resided at 2, Monmouth Court, the old woman and Julia worked at a small hand press—I joined him about 1818—his father died before.—I understood Julia went astray—the Mother Died about 1826. Anne Ryle was the widow of an Officer: a Waterloo man—with one child—had a pension.

Catnach had but little type, and no stock to speak of; he had a Sister at Portsea the wife of a mate of a ship in harbour, and kept a song-shop. His Mother lived with him 7 or 8 years.—I understand about the "Horses-heads." Cox and Kean, I forget except the title and chorus:—

COX versus KEAN;
OR
LITTLE BREECHES.

"With his ginger tail he did assail, and did the prize obtain,
This Merry Little Wanton Bantam Cock of Drury Lane—
LITTLE BREECHES."

Ann Stanton was tried for cutting the Cock's Head off there was no verses.

As regards the Sausages, Catnach printed a few lines on a quarter-sheet, that caused a great uproar, he was taken to Bow Street. Catnach had six months. There was no verses, it was quickly done. He printed the life of Mother Cummins, of Dyot Street—now, George Street, and that was knocked into "pye" in quick sticks. There was a change after he went to Alnwick in Northumberland, where he carried a small press and printed the state of the poll every day, while there he took up his freedom.* He came home and printed "Cubitt's Treadmill":—

"And we're all treading, tread, tread, treading,
And we're all treading at fam'd Brixton Mill."

and kept going forward—retired and went to Barnet, left the business to James Paul and Ann Ryle. That is many years ago. I seldom go near the Seven Dials, perhaps once in 3, 4, 5, or six months. I remember many occurrances but 56 years is a long time, I have just entered my 77th year. Anything you require as far as I can I will send and remain,

Yours Sincerely, Seovl

John Morgan

Charles Hindley, Esq.,
76, Rose Hill Terrace, Brighton.

---

* This is an error—See page 76.

xxvii.

1 Model Cottages, Little Ann's Lane,
Great Peter Street, Westminster, London, S.W.
29th February, 1876.

Dear Sir :—

If I was to go back and think of passing events it would fill a volume. First in 1820—Catnach then being very poor—at the death of George the third, and the Duke of Kent he printed an Elegy :

"Mourn, Britons mourn ! Your sons deplore,
Our royal Sovereign is now no more."

Then comes the election for Westminster : Burdett, Hobhouse, and Lamb. He had a song :—

"Oh, Cammy Hobby is the man,
And so is daddy Sir Franky, O ;
The Hon. W. Lamb is going mad
And kicking like a donkey, O."

"Oh, the naughty Lamb—
The miserable sinner, O
We'll have him roast and boil'd
And cut him up for dinner, O."

During the whole time of the election party spirit ran very high. A real lamb's head with a real rat in its mouth, was stuck upon the top of a pole. From the rat's tail hung a cock's comb. On the lamb's head was placed a lawyer's wig, surmounted with a fool's cap. On a board immediately below the head, was inscribed in front—"Behold the ratting lamb, with a cock's comb at his tail." On the other side, the inscription was—

"If silly lambs will go ratting,
'Tis fit they get this sort of batting."*

Then came The Dog's Meat Man—Founded on fact :—

IN Gray's Inn Lane, not long ago.
An old maid lived a life of woe ;
She was fifty-three, with a face like tan,
When she fell in love with a dogs'-meat man.
Much she loved this dogs'-meat man,
He was a good-looking dogs'-meat man ;
Her roses and lilies were turn'd to tan,
When she fell in love wi' the dogs'-meat man.

Every morning when he went by,
Whether the weather was wet or dry,
And right opposite her door he'd stand,
And cry "dogs'-meat," did this dogs'-meat man.
Then her cat would run out to the dogs'-meat man,
And rub against the barrow of the dogs'-meat man,
As right opposite to her door he'd stand,
And cry "Dogs' Meat, did this dogs'-meat man.

---

* The numbers at the close of **the Poll on** Saturday, 24th March, at three o'clock, stood as under :—

Sir Francis Burdett...................... 5,327
J. Cam Hobhouse, Esq................... 4,884
Hon. W. Lamb 4,436

xxviii.

He said his customers, good lord!
Owed him a matter of two pound odd;
And she replied, it was quite scan-
Dalous to cheat such a dogs'-meat man.
"If I had but the money," says the dogs'-meat man,
"I'd open a tripe-shop," says the dogs'-meat man,
"And I'd marry you to-morrow."—She admired the plan,
And she lent a *five-pound note* to the dogs'-meat man.

He pocketed the money and went away,
She waited for him all next day,
But he never com'd; and then she began
To think she was diddled by the dogs'-meat man;
She went to seek this dogs'-meat man,
But she couldn't find the dogs'-meat man;
Some friend gave her to understan'
He'd got a wife and seven children—this dogs'-meat man.

Mother Cummins lived and kept Brothels in Dyot Street, Bloomsbury Square, after, and still called George Street, named after the Prince Regent George 4th, at that time "Beggar's Opera" where the Prince and nobles resorted was at the Rose and Crown, Church Lane, St. Giles. Catnach printed her life. In the Beggar's Opera, were assembled matchmakers, beggars, prigs and all the lowest of the low. There was old black Billy Waters, with his wooden leg, dancing and playing his fiddle, and singing:—

Polly will you marry me—Polly don't you cry,
Polly come to bed with me; and get a little boy.

some were dipping matches, some boiling potatoes and **salt herrings, some** swearing, some dancing—all manners of fun, &c.

Then comes Queen Caroline's trial; Catnach gets out a song:—

As I walked down the Greenwich-road one evening in June,
I never saw so fine a sight as on that afternoon.
I never saw so fine a sight, or, one half so good,
As for to see Queen Caroline supported by a Wood.
That Wood shall never be cut down, but stand for ever more;
And he'll protect our innocent Queen Sweet Caroline on our shore.

which was followed by a skit on George 1Vth called:—

"THE GREAT BABE IN A MESS."

then another **on** Queen Caroline's *crin con* **case** with Bergami who couldn't *remember* nothing at all.

"BERGAMI, THE *Non mi recordo.*"

xxix.

Who are you? "*Non mi recordo.*"

What countryman are you—a foreigner or an Englishman? "*Non mi recordo.*"

There was something fresh everyday until the end of the Trial. Catnach then prints some "papers" belonging to J. Pitts, Printer, Gt. Saint Andrew-street, which causes a flare-up and a bother.

Then comes the sheet of "Horses Heads" which heads were like Eldon, Peel, Canning, &c. Just before they were out Mr. Rockcliff, a Printer in Old Gravel Lane, Radcliff-Highway sends for me—there was bottles of whisky. Rockcliff had engaged with a man called Oliver Cromwell to get him one of the first sheets printed off Catnach's press of the "Horses Heads" and he would give him half-a-crown. Rockcliff then requested me to bring him the first sheet of "Horses Heads" and get the half-a-crown. I went and got the sheet and meets Oliver Cromwell going into Catnach's as I came out, so I got the half-a-crown. Rockcliff copies the sheet, then engaged with Lowe the Printer in Compton-street to supply all the West-end. So it went on and made plenty of bother between them.

Catnach got on like a house on fire printing Religious Sheets, then came the murder of William Weare Esq. by John Thurtell, Hunt and Probert. I remember all that affair well,—Then the execution of Thurtell. A twelve-month after Probert was hanged for horsestealing. Then came the trial of Henry Fauntleroy a banker in Berner's Street Oxford Street executed for forgery. Then came Corder and Maria Marten and the Red Barn, so that is the way Catnach got on from a poor man to be a gentleman. There is many little things I may think of but close for the present and remain:—

Yours Humble Servt

John Morgan

XXX.

1, Model Cottages, Little St. Ann's Lane,
Great Peter Street, Westminster,
London. 17th March, 1876.

Sir,
I received yours. My recollection is not so good as I would wish.

I think to the best of my recollection in 1819 there were some old men who had been forty-years in the streets at that time, their names were old Jack Smith, Tom Caton, old Jack Rush, Tom Anderson and a few others. When they wanted anything they made up fresh reports, and things were done without the least hesitation. As respects Mr. Pizzy the Pork Butcher, it was some of these men that went to Blackman Street, Clare Market, and created an uproar about the sausages, crowds assembled, and windows were broken, they were charged with rioting and taken to Bow Street, before—as they told me, Sir Richard Burnie, and I think Mr. Minshull. Catnach was sent to Clerkenwell for trial, and was afterwards sentenced to six months, and he served the full time. Then there was the trial of the four poor Irishmen for coining, in the first year of the mayorality of the late Sir Matthew Wood, and a lot of other things which I think would answer the purpose.

About twenty-six years ago Henry Mayhew sent for me, and he began a a work something like yours, but by some means it stopped. There is matters that would help to fill up a Book without going to much expense.

Your Sincerely Servt
John Morgan

Charles Hindley, Esq.,
76, Rose Hill Terrace, Brighton.

At this date we were through the instrumentality of Mrs. Paul, widow of Mr. James Paul—formerly in the service of Catnach, introduced to Mrs. Elizabeth Benton, the last surviving daughter of John and Mary Catnach. Mr. Benton was assistant treasurer, and box-book keeper to Mr. Alfred Bunn, of Covent Garden and Drury Lane Theatres, Mrs. Benton, at the time being wardrobe-mistress and *costumier*. At one period Mr. and Mrs. Benton lived with Mr. Bunn in St James' Place, St. James' Street, Mrs. Benton acting in the capacity of housekeeper. During several seasons Mr. Benton was also treasurer for the proprietors of Vauxhall Gardens, afterwards he filled the same office for E. T. Smith— *Dazzle Smith !* at Cremorne Gardens. He died abroad in 1856. The interview we had with Mrs. Benton led up to receiving the two letters that follow :—

5, Sonderburg Road,
Seven Sisters' Road, Holloway.
London. *November,* 13*th,* 1876.

Dear Sir,

In reply to your letter, in which you ask if I know where my Father and mother were married, I regret to say I do not know for certain if it was in Edinburgh or Berwick-on-Tweed, but I am certain it was not in Alnwick.

* * * * * * * * *
* * * * * * * * *

I shall feel obliged for the [Alnwick] Journal, and also for the Register of Baptisms.

I always understood that my father was a descendant of Catnach, King of the Picts.

I remain
Yours &c
E. Benton

P.S.—The paper has not arrived—shall be glad to hear from you by return of Post.

Charles Hindley, Esq.,
  76, Rose Hill Terrace, Brighton.

xxxii.

5, Sonderburg Road,
Seven Sisters' Road, Holloway,
London. *November* 18, 1876.

Dear Sir,

I am sorry I have not answered your letter before, but I have been very ill.

I am sorry I can give you no more information than I have already given you, but about Mrs. Ryle and Mr.—— I cannot exactly say, and as my niece **Mrs. Harding was but a girl when her uncle died** I should not like to apply to her as it would be painful.

My father was dead when the Battle of Waterloo was fought, but was in Alnwick at the Battle of Trafalgar, and for **some time after.** My Father had 3 residences in London. 1. (only a shop) in Wardour Street, Soho Square, and ditto also Gerrard Street, and also in Charlotte Street, Fitzroy Square (apartments).

My Father had a **severe illness, also a fever of which he died.** I should feel very much obliged if you could find me a copy of the Hermit of Warkworth, and I will willingly pay for it, and also Blair's Grave.

I am very much obliged for the Registers, and if I can supply you with further information I will do so with pleasure. I have not heard from Mr. [Mark] Smith.

I remain
Yours &c
E Bintson

P.S.—I received the Paper [Alnwick Journal] with **thanks.**

C. Hindley, Esq.,
  76, Rose Hill Terrace, Brighton.

It was at this particular date of our history—1876—that we had the good fortune to get acquainted with Mr. George Skelly, of Alnwick—who, like ourselves, is possessed of the *cacoethes scribendi*, and was at the time supplying, *con amore*, an article to the *Alnwick Journal*, entitled "John and James Catnach," which we found to contain certain information relative to the elder Catnach, and also of the earlier portion of the life of James, of which we had no previous knowledge. At our solicitation to be allowed to make a selection from the same, we received a most courteous and gentlemanly letter, which, in addition to containing several pieces of information and answers to many queries we had put to Mr. Skelly, he wound up by saying :—" You have full liberty to make use of anything that I have written, and it will afford me much pleasure if I can further your intentions in any way"

From that date, Mr. George Skelly continued to correspond with us on the subject of the " Two Catnachs," nearly up to the last moment of our going to press with our own " Life and Times of James Catnach," and to him we are greatly indebted for much of the information therein contained. And it was at his suggestion that we wrote the following letter to the *Alnwick Journal*—Mr. Skelly at the same time furnishing the local paragraph.

Letter to the Editor.

To the Editor of the Alnwick Journal.

76, Rose Hill Terrace, Brighton,
June 16th, 1876.

SIR,—Your townsman, Mr. George Skelly, in the concluding chapter of his excellent article of " John and James Catnach," makes mention of my name as being engaged in preparing for publication " The Life and Times of James Catnach, formerly of Seven

Dials, printer of ballads, &c." Such being the fact, I shall therefore be glad if you would allow me sufficient space in the *Alnwick Journal*, to ask your readers and correspondents who possess any additional facts, sayings, doings, or letters of the two Catnachs—John and James—to supply me with the same, when I shall have much pleasure in assigning to any such contributions a proper chronological place in my work, and of acknowledging the source of the same, while all documents or books will be faithfully returned by yours, &c., &c.,

CHARLES HINDLEY.

JOHN AND JAMES CATNACH.—It will be seen by a correspondence in another page that Mr. Charles Hindley, of Brighton, is preparing for publication the "Life and Times of James Catnach," and he respectfully solicits from our readers any facts and scraps they may be possessed of, also the loan of any letters or books suitable for the extention of the life of the celebrated and withal eccentric printer, who, although a native of Alnwick, settled in London, and occupied a peculiar position for upwards of a quarter of a century in the Seven Dials district. We trust that our correspondent may be enabled to add to his all ready large stock of material in hand a few more items, by the publication of his letter in our columns. Mr. Hindley's work, will, it is expected, be published by Messrs. Reeves and Turner, of the Strand, London, during the coming autumn.

The above letter to the *Alnwick Journal* was the means of obtaining another valuable correspondent—Mr. George H. Thompson, also of Alnwick, who volunteered his services to aid and assist, to the best of his time and ability, in supplying all the information he possessed or could glean from his friends and acquaintances in the good old borough of Alnwick, or the county at large. And *inter alia* copied out *verbatim* from the Parish Register of Baptisms in St. Michael's Church all the entries in connection with the family of John and Mary Catnach and which will be found *in extenso* at pages 2-3 of this work.

Mr. George Skelly and Mr. G. H. Thompson are fortunate by their residence in Alnwick in having had the acquaintance and friendship of the late Mr. Mark Smith—James Catnach's fellow apprentice, Mr. Thomas Robertson, Mr. Tate, the local historian, and several other *Alnwick-folk*. And they have made the best possible use of the circumstance to supply us with information on the subject of our enquiry.

Recently Mr. Geo. Skelly has forwarded to us an original trade invoice of John Catnach of which we here append a *fac-simile* copy :—

We have now brought up the history of our pursuit of knowledge to the eve of the publication of the Life and Times of James Catnach—late of Seven Dials, Ballad-monger—which was first announced in 1878 in the manner following.

Ye Life of Jemmy Catnach.

Now, my friends, you have here just printed and pub—lish—ed, the Full, True, and Particular account of the Life, Trial, Character, Confession, Condemnation, and Behaviour, together with an authentic copy of the last 𝔚ill and 𝔗estament: or DYING SPEECH, of that eccentric individual "Old Jemmy Catnach," late of the *Seven Dials*, printer, publisher, toy-book manufacturer, dying-speech merchant, and ballad-monger. Here, you may read how he was bred and born the son of a printer, in the ancient Borough of Alnwick, which is in Northumberlandshire. How he came to London to seek his fortune. How he obtained it by printing and publishing children's books, the chronicling of doubtful scandals, fabulous duels between ladies of fashion, "cooked" assassinations, and sudden deaths of eminent individuals, apocryphal elopements, real or catch-penny accounts of murders, impossible robberies, delusive suicides, dark deeds and public executions, to which was usually attached the all-important and necessary "Sorrowful Lamentations," or, "Copy of Affectionate Verses," which, according to the established custom, the criminal composed, in the condemned cell, the night before his execution.

Yes, my customers, in this book you'll read how Jemmy Catnach made his fortune in Monmouth Court, which is to this day in the Seven Dials, which is in London. Not only will you read how he did make his fortune, but also what he did and what he didn't do with it after he had made it. You will also read how "Old Jemmy" set himself up as a fine gentleman :—JAMES CATNACH ES—QUIRE.

And how he didn't like it when he had done it. And how he went back again to dear old Monmouth Court, which is in the Seven Dials aforesaid. And how he languished, and languishing, did die—leaving all his old mouldy coppers behind him—and how being dead, he was buried in Highgate Cemetery.

Furthermore, my ready-money customers, you are informed that there are only 750 copies of the work print-ed and pub-lish-ed, viz., namely that is to say:—500 copies on crown 8vo, at 12/6 each. 250 copies on demy 8vo., at 25/- each.

LONDON:
REEVES AND TURNER,
196, STRAND, W.C.

1878.

xxxvii.

The Seven Dials!—Jemmy Catnach and Street Literature are, as it were, so inseparably bound together that we now propose to give a short history of the former to enable us to connect our own history with the later :—

The Seven Dials were built for wealthy tenants, and Evelyn, in his *Diary*, 1694, notes : " I went to see the building near St. Giles's, where Seven Dials make a star from a Doric pillar placed in the middle of a circular area, in imitation of Venice." The attempt was not altogether in vain. This part of the parish has ever since " worn its *dirt* with a difference." There is an air of shabby gentility about it. The air of the footman or waiting-maid can be recognised through the tatters, which are worn with more assumption than those of their unsophisticated neighbours.

> " You may break, you may shatter the vase if you will ;
> But the scent of the roses will hang round it still."

The Seven Dials are thus described in **Gay's Trivia** :—

> " Where famed St. Giles's ancient limits spread,
> An in-railed column rears its lofty head ;
> Here to seven streets, seven dials count their day,
> And from each other catch the circling ray ;
> Here oft the peasant, with inquiring face,
> Bewildered, trudges on from place to place ;
> He dwells on every sign with stupid gaze—
> Enters the narrow alley's doubtful maze—
> Tries every winding court and street in vain,
> And doubles o'er his weary steps again."

This column was removed in July, 1773, on the supposition that a considerable sum of money was lodged at the base ; but the search was ineffectual

Charles Knight, in his "London," writes thus of Seven Dials:—

"It is here that the literature of St. Giles's has fixed its abode; and a literature the parish has of its own, and that, as times go, of a very respectable standing in point of antiquity. In a letter from Letitia Pilkington, to the demure author of 'Sir Charles Grandison,' and published by the no less exemplary and irreproachable Mrs. Barbauld, the lady informs her correspondent that she has taken apartments in Great White Lion Street, and stuck up a bill intimating that all who have not found 'reading and writing come by nature,' and who had had no teacher to make up the defect by art, might have 'letters written here.' With the progress of education, printing presses have found their way into St. Giles's, and what with literature and a taste for flowers and birds, there is much of the 'sweet south' about the Seven Dials harmonising with the out-of-door habits of its occupants. It was here—in Monmouth Court, a thoroughfare connecting Monmouth Street with Little Earl Street—that the late eminent Mr. Catnach developed the resources of his genius and trade. It was he who first availed himself of greater mechanical skill and a larger capital than had previously been employed in the department of THE TRADE, to substitute—for the excrable tea-paper, blotched with lamp-black and oil, which characterised the old broadside and ballad printing—tolerably white paper and real printer's ink. But more than that, it was he who first conceived and carried into effect, the idea of publishing collections of songs by the yard, and giving to purchasers, for the small sum of one penny (in former days the cost of a single ballad), strings of poetry, resembling in shape and length the list of Don Juan's mistresses, which Leporello unrolls on the stage before Donna Anna. He was no ordinary man, Catnach; he patronised original talents in many a bard of St Giles's and is understood to have accumulated the largest store of broadsides, last dying speeches, ballads and other stock-in-trade of the flying stationer's upon record."

Douglas Jerrold in his article on the Ballad Singer, published in "Heads of the People; or Portraits of the English"—1841, writes thus of Seven Dials and its surroundings:—

"The public ear has become dainty, fastidious, hypercritical; hence the Ballad-Singer languishes and dies. Only now and then, his pipings are to

xxxix.

be heard   *   *   *   With the fall of Napoleon, declined the English Ballad-Singer. During the war, it was his peculiar province to vend halfpenny historical abridgments to his country's glory; recommending the short poetic chronicle by some familiar household air, that fixed it in the memory of the purchaser, who thus easily got hatred of the French by heart, with a new assurance of his own invulnerability. No battle was fought, no vessel taken or sunken, that the triumph was not published, proclaimed in the national gazette of our Ballad-Singer. If he were not the clear silver trump of Fame, he was at least her tin horn. It was he who bellowed music into news, which, made to jingle, was thus, even to the weakest understanding, rendered portable. It was his narrow strips of history that adorned the garrets of the poor; it was he who made them yearn towards their country, albiet to them so rough and niggard a mother.

Napoleon lost Waterloo, and the English Ballad-Signer not only lost his greatest prerogative, but was almost immediately assailed by foreign rivals, who had well-nigh played him dumb. Little thought the Ballad-Singer, when he crowed forth the crowning triumphs of the war, and in his sweetest possible modulations breathed the promised blessings of a golden peace, that he was then, swan-like, singing his own knell; that he did but herald the advent of his own provençal destroyers.

Oh muse! descend and say, did no omen tell the coming of the fall? Did no friendly god give warning to the native son of song? Burned the stars clearly, tranquilly in heaven,—or shot they madly across Primrose-hill, the Middlesex Parnassus?

    *   *   *   *   *   *   *   *   *

Evening had gathered o'er Saint Giles's, and Seven Dials. So tranquil was the season, even publishers were touched. Catnach and Pitts sat silent in their shops; placing their hands in breeches-poke, with that serenity which pockets best convey, they looked around their walls— walls more richly decked than if hung with triumphs of Sidonian looms, arrayed with Bayeux stitchings; walls, where ten thousand thousand ballads —strips harmonious, yet silent as Apollo's unbraced strings,—hung pendulous, or crisply curling, like John Braham's hair. Catnach and Pitts, the tuneful masters of the gutter-choir, serenely looked, yet with such comprehensive glance, that look did take their stock. Suddenly, more suddenly than e'er the leaves in Hornsey wood were stirred by instant blast, the thousand thousand ballads swung and rustled on the walls; yet wind there was not, not the lightest breath. Still like pendants fluttering in a northern breeze, the ballads streamed towards Catnach, and towards Pitts! Amazing truth—yet more; **each** ballad found a voice! 'Old Towler' faintly growled; 'Nancy Dawson' sobbed and sighed; and, 'Bright Chanticleer' crowed weakly, dolorously, as yet in chickenhood, and smitten with the pip. At the same instant, the fiddle, the antique viol of Roger Scratch, fell from its garret-peg, and lay shivered, even as glass.

A cloud fell upon Seven Dials; dread and terror chilled her many minstrels: and why—and wherefore?

At that dread moment, a ministrel from the sunny south, with barrel-organ, leapt on Dover beach! Seven Dials felt the shock: her troubadours, poor native birds, were to be out-carrolled and out-quavered, by Italian opera retailed by penn'orths to them, from the barrel-organs: and prompt to follow their masters, they let the English ballad singer sing unheard.

The Ballad-Singer has lost his occupation; yet should he not pass away unthanked, unrecompensed. We have seen him a useful minister in rude society; we have heard him a loud-mouthed advocate of party zeal, and we have seen him almost ground into silence by the southern troubadour. Yet was he the first music-seller in the land. Ye well-stocked, flourishing vendors of fashionable scores, deign to cast a look through plate glass at your poor, yet great original, bare-footed and in rags, singing, unabashed, amidst London wagon-wheels: behold the true decendant of the primative music-seller."

Charles **Dickens**, as Boz, long since "sketched" the Seven Dials, and at the same time and place given us his—" Meditations in Monmouth Street :—

" Seven Dials! the region of song and poetry—first effusions, and last dying speechees: hallowed by the names of Catnach and Pitts—names that will entwine themselves with costermongers, and barrel-organs, when penny magazines shall have superseded penny yards of song, and capital punishment be unknown."

xli.

Several years ago Mr. Albert Smith, who lived at Chertsey, discovered in his neighbourhood part of the Seven Dials—the column doing duty as a monument to a Royal Duchess—when he described the circumstance in a pleasant paper, entitled "Some News of a famous Old Fellow," in his "Town and Country Magazine." The communication is as follows:—

"Let us now quit the noisome mazes of St. Giles's and go out and away into the pure leafy country. Seventeen or eighteen miles from town, in the county of Surrey, is the little village of Weybridge.

One of the lions to be seen at Weybridge is Oatlands, with its large artificial grotto and bath-room, which is said—but we cannot comprehend the statement—to have cost the Duke of Newcastle, who had it built, £40,000. The late Duchess of York died at Oatlands, and lies in a small vault under Weybridge Church, wherein there is a monument, by Chantrey, to her memory. She was an excellent lady, well-loved by all the country people about her, and when she died they were anxious to put up some sort of a tribute to her memory. But the village was not able to offer a large some of money for this purpose. The good folks did their best, but the amount was still very humble, so they were obligated to dispense with the service of any eminent architect, and build up only such a monument as their means could compass. Someone told them that there was a column to be sold cheap in a stonemason's yard, which might answer their purpose. It was accordingly purchased; a coronet was placed upon its summit; and the memorial was set up on Weybridge Green, in front of the Ship Inn, at the junction of the roads leading to Oatlands, to Shepperton Lock, and to Chertsey. This column turned out to be the original one from Seven Dials.

The stone on which the dials were engraved or fixed, was sold with it. The poet Gay, however, was wrong when he spoke of its seven faces. It is hexagonal in its shape; this is accounted for by the fact that two of the streets opened into one angle. It was not wanted to assist in forming the monument, but was turned into a stepping stone, near the adjoining inn, to assist the infirm in mounting their horses, and there it now lies, having sunk by degrees into the earth; but its original form can still be easily surmised. It may be about three feet in diameter.

The column itself is about thirty feet high and two feet in diameter, displaying no great architectural taste. It is surmounted by a coronet, and the base is enclosed by a light iron railing. An appropriate inscription on one side of the base indicates its erection in the year 1822, on the others are some lines to the memory of the Duchess.

Relics undergo strange transpositions. The obelisk from the mystic solitudes of the Nile to the centre of the Place de la Concorde, in bustling Paris—the monuments of Nineveh to the regions of Great Russell Street—the frescoes from the long, dark, and silent Pompeii to the bright and noisy Naples—all these are odd changes. But in proportion to their importance, not much behind them is that old column from the crowded dismal regions of St. Giles to the sunny tranquil Green of Weybridge."

We are now approaching—" The beginning of the end "—of our history. We were not taken by surprise as we know that " coming events cast their shadows before," and that :—

> Often do the spirits
> Of great events stride on before the events,
> And in to-day already walks to-morrow.

Therefore we were well prepared to read in the newspapers of October, 1883, the following paragraph :—

> The old-established printing and publishing house formerly occupied by James Catnach, 2, Monmouth-court, Seven Dials, will soon be amongst the lost landmarks of London. The Metropolitan Board of Works have purchased the house, and it is to be pulled down to make the new street from Leicester-square to New Oxford-street. The business of the literature of the street was founded by James Catnach in 1813, who retired in 1840. The ballads and broadsides he printed, many of them illustrated with cuts by Bewick, helped to furnish the people with news and political and social ballads for generations.

All that is fortold in the above has since taken place, Monmouth-court and the house and shop wherein old Jemmy Catnach established the "Catnach Press" in the year 1813 has disappeared to make way for the "New Thoroughfare" from Leicester-square to New Oxford street, and :—

THE CATNACH PRESS

removed by Mr. W. S. Fortey—Catnach's successor—to Great St. Andrew-street, Bloomsbury, W.C.

O tempora ! O mores !

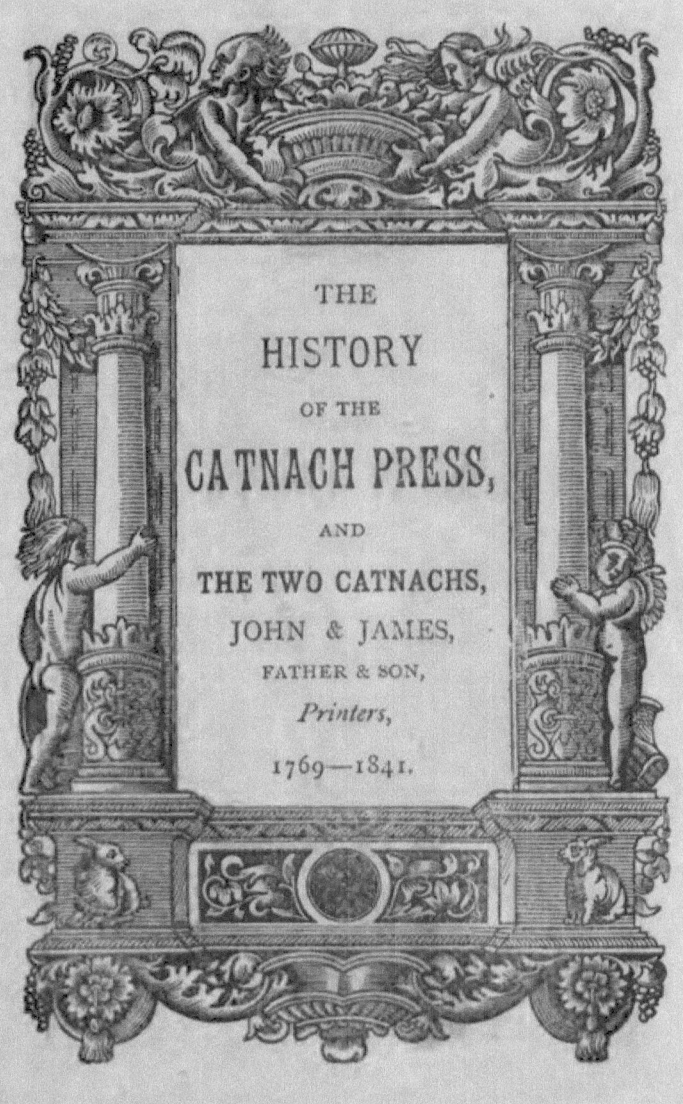

THE HISTORY OF THE CATNACH PRESS, AND THE TWO CATNACHS, JOHN & JAMES, FATHER & SON, *Printers*, 1769—1841.

THOMAS BEWICK,

Thomas Bewick died at his house on the Windmill-Hills, Gateshead, November the 8th, 1828, in the seventy-sixth year of his age, and on the 13th he was buried in the family burial-place at Ovingham, where his parents, wife, and brother were interred.

THE CATNACH PRESS.

———o———

In addition to the full title of our work—"The History of the Catnach Press"—the two Catnachs—John and James—father and son, we deem it necessary to incidentally introduce into our pages some notice of Alnwick, an ancient borough, market-town and parish of Northumberland, also a few passing remarks on the life and doings of Mr. William Davison, who, in conjunction with the elder Catnach as a business partner and subsequent successor, employed Thomas Bewick—an English artist, who imparted the first impulse to the art of wood-engraving—for many of their publications.

Of the early life of John Catnach, *(Kat-nak)*, the father, we have little information. He was born in 1769, at Burntisland, a royal burgh and parish of Fifeshire, Scotland, where his father was possessed of some powder-mills. The family afterwards removed to Edinburgh, when their son John was bound apprentice to his uncle, Sandy Robinson, the printer. After having duly served out his indentures, he worked for some short time in Edinburgh, as a journeyman, then started in a small business of his own in Berwick-upon-Tweed, where he married

Mary Hutchinson, who was a native of Dundee, a seaport-town in Scotland. While at Berwick a son and heir, John, was born. In 1790 they removed their business to Alnwick, and during their residence there seven children were born to them and from the Register of Baptisms in St. Michael's Church we glean that four of them were baptised at one time, viz., September 24, 1797, and there described as "of John Catnach, printer, and Mary his wife: Dissenter." [?] John Catnach had been brought up in the Roman Catholic faith, and his wife as a Presbyterian. The following is taken *vertabim* from the Parish Register:—

Sep^t. 24, 1797.
Margaret, Daug^r. of John Catnach, printer, and Mary his Wife. Born Decr. 26th, 1790. Dissenter.

James, son of John Catnach, printer, and Mary his Wife. Born August 18th, 1792. Dissenter.

Mary, Daug^r. of John Catnach, printer, and Mary his Wife. Born February 26th, 1794. Dissenter.

Nancy, Daug^r. of John Catnach, printer, and Mary his Wife. Born Sepr. 2nd. 1795. Dissenter.

May 23, 1798.
Elizabeth Catnach. Born March 21, 1797, 4th Daughter of John Catnach, printer, native of Burnt Island, Shire of Fife, by his wife Mary Hutchinson, Native of Dundee, Angus Shire, Scotland.

Decr. 14, 1798.
Isabella Catnach. Born Novr. 2, 1798. 5th Daughter of Jno. Catnach, Stationer, Nat. of Scotland, by his wife, Mary Hutchinson, Nat. of Dundee, Angus Shire, Scotland.

March 28, 1800.

Jane Catnach, 6th Daughter of John Catnach, printer, Native of Edinburgh *(sic)* by his wife Mary Hutchinson, Native of Dundee, Scotland.

To the above we have to add that there were two sons—John, born to John and Mary Catnach. John I. who was born at Berwick-upon-Tweed, died August 27, 1794, aged 5 years and 7 months, and we find him duly recorded in the Register of Deaths. John II., whose name appears at the end of the inscription on a tombstone in Alnwick churchyard, and of which further mention will be made in another portion of our work, died, presumably unbaptized, March 5, 1803, aged 4 months.

John Catnach was not long a resident in the borough of Alnwick before he became acquainted with many of the principal tradesmen in the place. Naturally he was of a free-and-easy disposition, and, like many of his kinsman on the Borders, was particularly fond of the social glass. The latter practice he allowed to grow upon him in such a way that it ultimately interfered very much with his business prospects, and finally hastened his death.

The shop that he commenced business in, was situated in Narrowgate-street, and adjoining the old Half-Moon hostelry. In gaining access to the place one had to ascend a flight of steps. Whilst in this shop he secured a fair amount of patronage, and the specimens of printing that emanated from his press are of such a character as to testify to his qualifications and abilities in the trade which he adopted as his calling. He possessed a fond regard for the traditions and customs which for centuries had been so closely associated with the Border country.

When the printing press was first introduced into Alnwick is not exactly known; but that it was considerably before the time of Catnach is certain. John Vint, the bookseller and author of the "Burradon Ghost," for several years used a press for printing purposes in the town, and Thomas Lindsay carried on a similar business at a still earlier period.

John Catnach had a great relish for printing such works as would admit of expensive embellishments, which, at the time he commenced business, were exceedingly rare. The taste he displayed in the execution of his work will be best exemplified in examining some of the printed editions of the standard works which emanated from his press; and in no instance is this more characteristically set forth than in those finely printed books which are so beautifully illustrated by the masterly hand of Thomas Bewick and his accomplished and talented pupil, Luke Clennell. Notably among which are:—

1.—"The Beauties of Natural History. Selected from Buffon's History of Quadrupeds, &c. Alnwick: J. Catnach, [n. d.] *Circa* 1790, 12mo., pp. 92. With 67 cuts by Bewick."—Another edition. Published and Sold by the Booksellers. By Wilson and Spence, York, and J. Catnach, printer, Alnwick. (Price 1s. 6d. sewed, or 2s. half-bound.) [n. d.] *Circa* 1795.

The embellishments of "The Beauties of Natural History" form an unique and valuable collection. They are very small and were done at an exceedingly low price, yet every bird and animal is exquisitely brought out in the minutest detail; whilst many of the illustrations which served as "tail pieces" are gems of art.

2.—"Poems by Percival Stockdale. With cuts by Thomas Bewick. Alnwick: printed by J. Catnach. 1800."

3.—"The Hermit of Warkworth. A Northumberland Ballad. In three Fits. By Dr. Thos. Percy, Bishop of Dromore. With Designs by Mr. Craig; and Engraved on Wood by Mr. Bewick. Alnwick: Printed and Sold by J. Catnach. Sold by Lackington, Allen, and Co., London; Constable and Co., Edinburgh; and Hodgson, Newcastle. 1806." The Arms of the Duke of Northumberland precedes the Dedication, thus:—

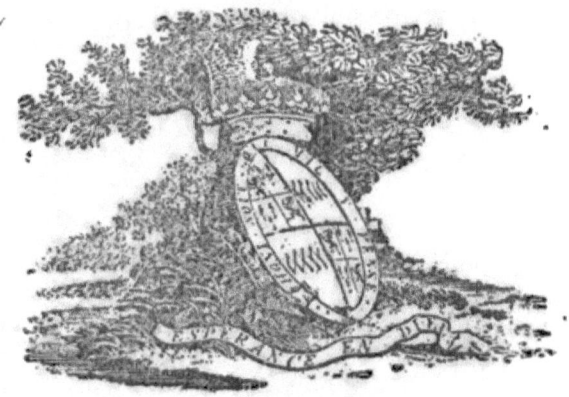

TO HER GRACE
FRANCES JULIA,
DUCHESS OF NORTHUMBERLAND,
This Edition of
THE HERMIT OF WARKWORTH,
Is respectfully Inscribed
By Her Grace's Obliged and Humble Servant,
J. CATNACH

ALNWICK, *October*, 1805.

4.—"A Second Edition; of which a few copies were printed on extra thick paper, royal 8vo., to match with some of his other works, illustrated by Bewick, pp. xiv., 182, with 13 cuts. At the end of the Poem are a Postcript, a Description of the Hermitage of Warkworth, Warkworth Castle, Alnwick Castle, Alnwick Abbey, and A Descriptive Ride in Hulne Park, Alnwick: Printed and Sold by J. Catnach. Sold by Wilson and Spence, York. 1807.

THE HERMIT OF WARKWORTH.

"And now, attended by their host,
The hermitage they view'd."

With hospitable haste he rose,
And wak'd his sleeping fire:
And snatching up a lighted brand,
Forth hied the reverend sire.

* * * *

He fought till more assistance came ;
   The Scots were overthrown ;
Thus freed me, captive, from their bands,
   To make me more his own.

The illustrations of "The Hermit of Warkworth" are, upon the whole, very creditable, and are well calculated to enhance the value of the book, but as works of art some few of them fall far short of many of Craig or Bewick's other productions.

John Catnach also printed and published a series of Juvenile Works, as "The Royal Play Book: or, Children's Friend. A Present for Little Masters and Misses." "The Death and Burial of Cock Robin, &c. ADORNED with CUTS.—Which in many cases were the early productions of Thomas Bewick.—Alnwick: Sold Wholesale and Retail by J. Catnach, at his Toy-Book Manufactory."

In the year 1807, John Catnach took an apprentice—a lad named Mark Smith, of whom more anon; a few months afterwards he entered into partnership with a Mr. William Davison, who was a native of Ponteland, in the county of Northumberland, but he duly served his apprenticeship as a chemist and druggist to Mr. Hind, of Newcastle-upon-Tyne, and for whom he ever cherished a fond regard. The union was not of long duration—certainly under two years—but it is very remarkable that two such men should have been brought together, for experience has shown that they were both morally and socially, the very opposite of each other.

During the partnership: Mr. Davison held his business of chemist, &c., in Bondgate-street; while the printing and publishing continued at Narrowgate-street, and among the works published by the firm of CATNACH and DAVISON we may record:—

"The Minstrel; or, The Progress of Genuis. In Two Parts. With some other Poems. By James Beattie, LL.D. With sixteen Cuts from Designs by Mr. Thurston; and engraved on Wood by Mr. Clennel, Alnwick. Printed by Catnach and Davison. Sold by the Booksellers in England and Scotland. 1807. 12mo. and Royal 8vo., pp 142."

"The Grave. A Poem. By Robert Blair. To which is added Gray's Elegy. In a Country Church Yard. With Notes Moral and Explanatory. Alnwick: Printed by Catnach and Davison. Sold by the Booksellers in England, Scotland, and Ireland. 1808. 12mo., pp. xiv., 72. With a frontispiece and other cuts by Thomas Bewick."

THE GRAVE.

"Prone, on the lowly grave of the dear man
  She drops; whilst busy meddling Memory,
In barbarous succession, musters up
  The past endearments of their softer hours
Tenacious of its theme."

After the dissolution of the strange partnership, Mr. Davison still prosecuted with vigour the several departments of the business; for although reared to the prescribing of physics, he had a fine taste and relish for the book trade, and the short time that he was with Catnach enabled him to acquire a good amount of valuable information on this subject. Be this as it may, he soon laid the basis of a large and lucrative business. About the first work Mr. Davison issued on his own account was:—

THE REPOSITORY OF SELECT LITERATURE.

Being an Elegant Assemblage of Curious, Scarce, Entertaining and Instructive Pieces in Prose and Verse. Adorned with beautiful Engravings by Bewick, &c. Alnwick: Printed by W. Davison. Sold by the Booksellers in England and Scotland. 1808.

This work is a fine specimen of provincial book-printing; its pages are adorned with some of Bewick's excellent cuts. There is one that we would particularly refer to, and that is "Shepherd Lubin." In size it is very small, but, like most of Bewick's pieces, sufficiently large to show the inimitable skill of the artist. The picture tells its own tale :—

> " Young Lubin was a shepherd's boy,
> Who watched a rigid master's sheep,
> And many a night was heard to sigh,
> And may a day was seen to weep."

———o———

And for whole days would wander in those places she had been used to walk with Henry.

"The History of Crazy Jane, by Sarah Wilkinson, with a frontispiece by Bewick: Alnwick. Printed by W. Davison; *and Sold by all the Principal Booksellers in England and Scotland.* 1813."

"Willie Brew'd a Peck o'Maut."

"The Poetical Works of Robert Burns. Engravings on Wood by Bewick, from designs by Thurston. Alnwick: Printed by Catnach and Davison, 1808." And London: Printed for T. Cadell and Davis, Strand, 1814. With cuts previously used in Davison's publications.

"Many of the engravings produced for Burns' Poems, are of a very superior class, and cannot be too highly commended."—*Hugo*.

"Sandie and Willie."

"The Poetical Works of Robert Ferguson, with his Life. Engravings on Wood by Bewick. ALNWICK: Printed by W. Davison."

Mr. Davison, following up the actions of his former partner, had a great regard for the standard poets. Previous to the issuing of the poems of Ferguson they had tried to imbue a better taste into the minds of the general reader, by means of publishing nothing but what was of an elevating character. And this will be seen by examining such works as Buffon, Beattie, Percy, Burns, &c. Almost simultaneously with the poems of Burns appeared those of Ferguson. Both works are uniform in size and price—*viz:* 2 vols, Foolscap 8vo.—12s. in boards; they contain some of Bewick's choicest and most exquisite wood-engravings.

"The Northumberland Minstrel: A Choice Selection of Songs. Alnwick: Printed by W. Davison."

There were only three numbers of this work published,* each of which contained 48 pages. The object of this undertaking was for the carrying out a project which at that time was becoming very popular, and consisted in bringing together in a collected form some of the best and most admired of our ballad-poetry. In fact, the object Mr. Davison had in view was only to extend what had been so successfully accomplished by Herd, Ramsay, Motherwell, Ritson, and others.

Mr. Davison continued in business at Alnwick up to the time of his death, in 1858, at the ripe age of 77. He was by far the most enterprising printer that had settled in the North of England. His collection of wood blocks was very large, and it is hardly possible to form an adequate conception of the many hundreds of beautiful specimens which he possessed. He stated that he had paid Thomas Bewick upwards of five hundred pounds for various woodcut blocks. With a view of disposing of some of his surplus stock, he printed and published in 4to., a catalogue :—"NEW SPECIMENS OF CAST-METAL ORNAMENTS AND WOOD TYPES, SOLD BY W. DAVISON. ALNWICK. With impressions of 1,100 Cast Ornaments and Wood Blocks, many of the latter executed by Thomas Bewick." This Catalogue—now exceedingly rare—is of the greatest interest and utility, as it embraces a series of cuts dispersed, as Mr. Hugo plainly shows, among a considerable number of publications, and enables those who collect Bewick's pieces to detect the hand of the Artist in many of his less elaborated productions.

---

* Mr. George Skelly—*Alnwick*.

Those of our readers who desire more information as to the many books printed by W. Davison, the Alnwick publisher, are referred to "The Bewick Collector," and the Supplement thereto, by the Rev. Thomas Hugo, M.A., &c. London: 1866—68. These volumes, illustrated by upwards of two hundred and ninety cuts, comprise an elaborate descriptive list of the most complete collection yet formed of the works of the renowned wood-engravers of Newcastle-upon-Tyne. Not only to Bewick collectors, but to all persons interested in the progress of Art, and especially of wood-engraving, these volumes, exhibiting chronologically the works of the Fathers of that Art in England, cannot fail to be of the highest interest.

Mr. Davison printed and published a series of Halfpenny Books; they are not only well printed, but in addition to this it is not unusual to see them illustrated by some of Thomas Bewick's choicest engravings. Mr. Hugo possessed twenty-seven in number, the titles of which he enumerates in his "Bewick Collector" and the Supplement thereto: adding the remarks that follow:—

> "The cuts in these little publications are for the most part the same which were used by Davison in the other and more important works which issued from his press. The volumes are in 32mo, and in typographical excellence are far in advance of all other children's books of the period of their publication with which I am acquainted."

Herewith we publish one of the series from our own private collection. The justness of Mr. Hugo's opinion will be at once seen.

THE

GUESS BOOK,

A COLLECTION OF

INGENIOUS PUZZLES.

ALNWICK:
Published and Sold by W. Davison.

Price One Halfpenny,

2

a b c d e

f g h i j k

l m n o p

q r s t u v

w x y z &

3

THE
GUESS BOOK.

THE MOON.

'There was a thing a full month old,
   When Adam was no more;
But ere that thing was five weeks old,
   Adam was years five score.

4

Guess Book.

A CAT.

In almost every house I'm seen,
   (No wonder then I'm common),
I'm neither man, nor maid, nor child,
   Nor yet a married woman.

5
Guess Book.

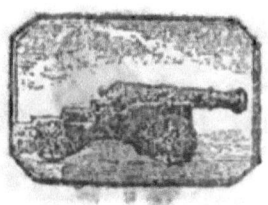

A CANNON.

I am the terror of mankind,
   My breath is flame, and by its power
I urge my messenger to find
   A way into the strongest tower.

6

Guess Book.

AN OWL.

My patron is Wisdom—if Wisdom you prize,
In me put your confidence, borrow my eyes,
Who into a mill-stone can see quite as far
As the best of you all, by the light of a star.

7

Guess Book.

A TOP.

I ne'er offend thee,
Yet thou dost me whip,
Which don't amend me,
Though I dance and skip;
When I'm upright,
Me you always like best,
And barbarously whip me
When I want rest.

8

Guess Book.

BOOKS.

With words unnumber'd I abound;
In me mankind do take delight;
In me much learning's to be found;
Yet I can neither read nor write.

9

Guess Book.

A DRUM.

My sides are firmly
Lac'd about,
Yet nothing is within :
You'll think my head
Is strange indeed,
Being nothing else but skin.

10

Guess Book.

A SAND-GLASS.

Made of two bodies join'd,
Without foot or hand;
And yet you will find
I can both run and stand.

11

Guess Book.

TIME.

Ever eating, never cloying,
All devouring, all destroying,
Never finding full repast
Till I eat the world at last.

12

Guess Book.

DEATH.

The gate of life, the cause of strife,
    The fruit of sin,
When I appear, you drop a tear,
    And stay within.

13

Guess Book.

A PAIR OF SHOES.

To rich and poor
We useful are ;
And yet for our reward,
By both at last
We're thrown away,
Without the least regard.

14

Guess Book.

A SQUIRREL.

I am a busy active creature,
Fashion'd for the sport of nature,
Nimbly skip from tree to tree,
Under a well-wrought canopy;
Bid Chloe then to Mira tell
What's my name and where I dwell.

15

Guess Book.

A FISH.

Though it be cold I wear no clothes,
  The frost and snow I never fear;
I value neither shoes nor hose,
  And yet I wander far and near.

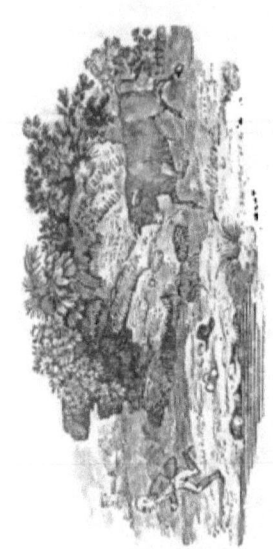

John Catnach

AT

NEWCASTLE.

———o———

"There is no fooling with Life, when it is once turned forty: the seeking of a Fortune then is but a desperate after-game: it is a hundred to one if a man fling three sixes, and recover all; if his hand be no luckier than mine."—*Cowley.*

In or about the latter part of the year 1808, John Catnach, with his wife and family, left Alnwick for Newcastle-upon-Tyne, and commenced business in a small shop in Newgate-street, and among other Works which he printed there, mention may be made of "The Battle of Chevy Chase," a selection from the works of "Dr. Samuel Johnson, in two volumes," and "The Life of John Thompson, Mariner. Written by Himself: Also, his Divine Selections, in Prose and Verse. *From esteemed Authors.* Embellished with steel Engravings. Newcastle: *Printed for the Author.* By J. Catnach, Newgate-street. 1810. 12mo., pp. lxxvi., 214. With two tail-pieces by Thomas Bewick."

John Thompson, *alias* Godfried Thomas Leschinsky, born at Riga, 1782, was a seaman. He sailed with Nelson's fleet to Copenhagen, 1801. Continuing at sea he endured many hardships from severe accidents and ill health, and was at length discharged as not being fit for his Majesty's service. In 1806, while in the Infirmary at Newcastle, one of his legs—from old injuries, rapidly mortified and had to be amputated. Subsequently, in consequence of the bones and joints of his right hand decaying, his arm was taken off below the elbow. He for years made a living out of his misfortunes and assumed piety. Catnach was induced, by specious reasoning, to undertake the printing of the book, but the eleemosynary author dying just as it was all worked off but not bound, he had the whole of the stock thrown on his hands to do the best he could with. There were between fifty and sixty claims set up by persons who averred that they had in part, or whole, paid for a copy each to the author on signing his subscription list, and most of these claims were allowed on the payment of sixpence extra: the work was subscribed for at 3s. 6d., but being extended to 20 pages more than was expected, the price was advanced to 4s.

John Catnach, at Newcastle, worked attentively for awhile, but without finding his expectations realised. Alas! time and the change of scene and companions had not improved the man. He contrived to get into a great amount of debt, without the least possible chance, from his irregular mode of living, of being able to pay it off. Eventually, he made up his mind for the worst, and the downward course would seem to have been the only way open to him. From bad to worse, and from one extreme to the other, he rapidly drifted. The loose and irregular manner in which he had existed was beginning to tell upon his constitution. His business had been neglected, and his adventures were nearly at a climax. The wreck came, with a terrific blow; but it was not unlooked for. Poor Catnach was a bankrupt, and as such sent to the debtor's gaol. But just before, he had managed to send his wife and daughters to London, together with a wooden printing press, some small quantity of type, and other articles of his trade that could be hurriedly and clandestinely got together.

During the five years' residence of John and Mary Catnach in Newcastle, they had one child, Isabella, burned to death, and another, Julia Dalton, born to them.

Mr. Mark Smith, who had been bound apprentice to John Catnach, but by reason of whose removal from the Borough of Alnwick, the indentures had been rendered void, was then in London, serving out his time as a turnover and improver with Mr. John Walker, of Paternoster Row, and on being made acquainted with the arrival of Mrs. Catnach and her family, paid them a visit at their lodgings in a court leading off Drury-lane, and assisted in putting up the press and arranging the other few matters and utensils in connection with their tiny printing office, there to await John Catnach's release from prison and arrival in the metropolis.

London life to John Catnach proved very disastrous, matters never went smoothly with him. It was evident to all his friends that he had made a great mistake in leaving the North of England. Mr. Mark Smith continued to visit the family as opportunities presented themselves. On one occasion he found them in extremely distressed circumstances, so much so, that he had to afford them some temporary relief from his slender earnings and then left the northern sojourners for the night, promising that he would return to see them at an early date. Anxious to learn how they were succeeding in the crowded metropolis, it was not many days before he again visited them, but this time he found them in a sorry plight; the landlady had distrained upon their all for arrears of rent. This was an awkward predicament; but the indomitable young Northumbrian, like the more burly Dr. Johnson of old, when his friend Oliver Goldsmith was similarly situated, resolved to do all he could to rescue him from the peril in which he was placed. Not being prepared for a case of such pressing emergency, the full debt and costs being demanded, he was compelled to borrow the required amount of Mr. Matthew Willoughby, a native and freeman of the Borough of Alnwick, then residing in London, and once more his old master was free.

John Catnach then removed his business to a front shop in Soho, when, in the absence of work of a higher class, he had to resort to printing quarter-sheet ballads, here is the title and imprint of one example :—

TOM STARBOARD AND FAITHFUL NANCY.

Tom Starboard was a lover true,
As brave a tar as ever sail'd ;
The duties ablest seamen do
Tom did, and never had fail'd.

* * * * *

LONDON.—Printed by J. Catnach, and Sold Wholesale and Retail at No. 60, Wardour-street, Soho-square.

For his wife and family he took apartments in Charlotte Street, Fitzroy-square. Again he shortly removed his business to Gerrard-street, where he had hardly got his plant into working order, when on returning home on the evening of the 29th of August, 1813, he had the misfortune to fall down and injure his leg. He was immediately taken to St. George's Hospital, Hyde-park Corner, when rheumatic fever supervened, and although placed under the skilful treatment of Dr. Young, he never rallied, his constitution being completely broken, but by means of superior medical treatment and good nursing he lingered until the 4th of December in the same year, on which day he died.

Such is a brief *résumé* of the latter years of John Catnach's life. It is apparent that, by a little application and self-denial, this man might have made for himself a name and position in the world. He possessed all the necessary talents for bringing success within his reach. The ground which he took is the same which in after years proved to be of inestimable value to hundreds of publishers who never possessed half the amount of ability and good taste in printing and embellishing books that was centred in him.

After his death, and just at the time when his widow and daughters were sunk in the greatest poverty, his son James, who in after years became so noted in street literature publications, made his way to the metropolis. It appears that this extraordinary man at one time contemplated devoting his life to rural pursuits; in fact, when a youth he served for some time as a shepherd boy, quite contrary to the wish and desire of his parents. Every opportunity he could get he would run away, far across the moors and over the Northumbrian mountains, and, always accompanied with his favourite dog Venus, and a common-place book, in which he jotted down in rhymes and chymes his notions of a pastoral life.* Thus he would stay away from home for days and nights together.

---

* At an interview which we had in 1877 with

E Benson

Née. Elizabeth Catnach, the last survivor of the family of John and Mary Catnach, she informed us that the MS. book alluded to above, remained in the family for many years, and was last known to be in the possession of the sister Mary—Mrs. Haines, of Gosport, to the date of about 1863.

This project, however, was abandoned, and he commenced to serve as a printer in the employment of his father. It is rather remarkable that he and Mr. Mark Smith

Mr. Smith,

were both bound on the same day as apprentices to Mr. John Catnach, and that they afterwards worked together as "improvers" in their trade with :—

Joseph Graham, Printer, Alnwick.

Mr. Hugo, in the Supplement to his "Bewick Collector," pp. 256 (5137), says :—"This very beautiful Cut was done by Thomas Bewick, sometime about the year 1794, for a well-known Alnwick printer."

THE HISTORY OF

James Catnach

> "Death made no conquest of this man,
> For now he lives in fame, though not in life."

At the time James—or, as he afterwards was popularly called "*Jemmy*," or, "*Old Jemmy*" Catnach commenced business in Seven Dials it took all the prudence and tact which he could command to maintain his position, as at that time "Johnny" Pitts,* of the Toy and Marble Warehouse, No. 6, Great St. Andrew street, was the acknowledged and established printer of street literature for the "Dials" district; therefore, as may be easily imagined, a powerful rivalry and vindictive jealousy soon arose between these "two of a trade"—most especially on the part of "Old Mother" Pitts, who is described as being a coarse and vulgar-minded personage, and as having originally followed the trade of a bumboat woman at Portsmouth: she "wowed wengeance" against the young fellow in the court for daring to set up in their business, and also spoke of him as a young "Catsnatch," "Catblock," "Cut-throat," and many other opprobrious terms which were freely given to the new comer. Pitts' staff of "bards" were duly cautioned of the conseqences which would inevitably follow should they dare to write a line for Catnach—the new *cove* up the court. The injunction was for a time obeyed, but the "Seven Bards of the Seven Dials" soon found it not only convenient, but also more profitable to sell

---

* Pitts, a modern publisher of love garlands, merriments, penny ballads,
    "Who, ere he went to heaven,
      Domiciled in Dials Seven!"—
            G. DANIEL'S "Democritus in London."

copies of their effusions to both sides at the same time, and by keeping their own counsel they avoided detection, as each printer accused the other of obtaining an early sold copy, and then reprinting it with the utmost speed, which was in reality often the case, as "Both Houses" had emissaries on the constant look-out for any new production suitable for street-sale. Now, although this style of "double dealing" and competition tended much to lessen the cost price to the "middle-man," or vendor, the public in this case did not get any of the reduction, as a penny broadside was still a penny, and a quarter-sheet still a halfpenny to them, the "street patterer" obtaining the whole of the reduction as extra profit.

The feud existing between these rival publishers, who have been somewhat aptly designated as the Colburn and Bentley of the "paper" trade, never abated, but, on the contrary, increased in acrimony of temper, until at last not being content to vilify each other by "Words! words!! words!!!" alone, they resorted to printing off virulent lampoons, in which Catnach never failed to let the world know that "Old Mother Pitts" had been formerly a bumboat woman, while the Pitt's party announced that :—

"All the boys and girls around,
    Who go out prigging rags and phials,
Know Jemmy *Catsnatch*!!! well,
    Who lives in a back slum in the Dials.
He hangs out in Monmouth Court,
    And wears a pair of blue-black breeches,
Where all the "Polly Cox's crew" do resort
    To chop their swag for badly printed Dying Speeches."

But however, in spite of all the opposition and trade rivalry, Catnach persevered; he worked hard, and lived hard, and was fitted to the stirring times. The Peninsular wars had just concluded, politics and party strife ran high, squibs, lampoons, and political ballads were the order of the day, and he made money. But he had weighty pecuniary family matters to bear up with, as thus early in his career, his father's sister also joined them, and they all lived and huddled together in the shop and parlour of No. 2, Monmouth-court. He did a small and very humble trade as a jobbing master, printing and publishing penny histories, street-papers, and halfpenny songs, relying for their composition on one or two out of the known "Seven Bards of the Seven Dials," and when they were on the drink, or otherwise not inclined to work, being driven to write and invent them himself.

The customers who frequented his place of business were for the most part of the lowest grades of society :—those who by folly, intemperance, and crime, had been reduced to the greatest penury. Anyone with a few coppers in his pockets could easily knock out an existence, especially when anything sensational was in the wind.

The great excitement throughout the country caused by the melancholy death of the Princess Charlotte, on the sixth day of November, 1817, was an event of no ordinary description. It was, indeed, a most unexpected blow, the shining virtues, as well as the youth and beauty of the deceased, excited an amount of affectionate commiseration, such as probably had never before attended the death of any royal personage in England.

The Seven Dials Press was busily engaged in working off "papers" descriptive of every fact that could be gleaned from the newspapers, and that was suitable for street sale. Catnach was not behind his compeers, as he published several statements in respect to the Princess's death, and *made* the following lines *out of his own head!* And had, continued our informant—a professional street-ballad writer—" *wood* enough left for as many more" :—

> "She is gone! sweet Charlotte's gone!
> Gone to the silent bourne;
> She is gone, She's gone, for evermore,—
> She never can return.
>
> She is gone with her joy—her darling Boy,
> The son of Leopold, blythe and keen;
> She Died the sixth of November,
> Eighteen hundred and seventeen."

The year 1818, proved a disastrous one to Catnach, as in addition to the extra burden entailed on him in family matters, he had, in the way of his trade, printed a street-paper reflecting on the private character and on the materials used in the manufacture of the sausages as sold by the pork butchers of the Drury-lane quarter in general, and particularly by Mr. Pizzey, a tradesman carrying on business in Blackmore-street, Claremarket, who caused him to be summoned to the Bow-street Police Court to answer the charge of malicious libel, when he was committed to take his trial at the next Clerkenwell Sessions, by Sir Richard Birnie, where he was sentenced to six months' imprisonment in the House of Correction, at Clerkenwell, in the County of Middlesex.

During Catnach's incarceration his mother and sisters, aided by

one of the Seven Dials bards, carried on the business, writing and printing off all the squibs and street ballads that were required. In the meanwhile the Johnny Pitts' crew printed several lampoons on "Jemmy Catnach." Subjoined is a portion of one of them that has reached us, *vivâ voce*, of the aforesaid—John Morgan—professional street-ballad writer :—

> "Jemmy Catnach printed a quarter sheet—
>   It was called in lanes and passages,
> That Pizzy the butcher, had dead bodies chopped,
>   And made them into sausages.
>
> " Poor Pizzey was in an awful mess,
>   And looked the colour of cinders—
> A crowd assembled from far and near,
>   And they smashed in all his windows.
>
> " Now Jemmy Catnach's gone to prison,
>   And what's he gone to prison for?
> For printing a libel against Mr. Pizzey,
>   Which was sung from door to door.
>
> " Six months in quod old Jemmy's got,
>   Because he a shocking tale had started,
> About Mr. Pizzey who dealt in sausages
>   In Blackmore-street, Clare-market."

Misfortunes are said never to come singly, and so it proved to the Catnach family, for while Jemmy was *doing* his six months in the House of Correction at Clerkenwell, we find in the pages of the *Weekly Dispatch* for January 3, 1819, and under POLICE INTELLIGENCE, as follows :—

CIRCULATING FALSE NEWS.—At Bow-street, on Wednesday, Thomas Love and Thomas Howlett, were brought to the office by one of the patrole, charged with making a disturbance in Chelsea, in the morning, by blowing of horns, with a tremendous noise, and each of them after blowing his horn, was heard to announce with all the vociferation the strength of his lungs would admit of :—" The full, true, and particular account of the most cruel and barbarous murder of Mr. Ellis, of Sloane-street, which took place, last night, in the Five Fields, Chelsea." The patrole, knowing that no such horrid event had taken place, had them taken up. The papers in their possession, which they had been selling at a halfpenny each, were seized and brought to the office with the prisoners. But what is most extraordinary, the contents of the papers had no reference whatever to Mr. Ellis! They were headed in large letters, " A HORRID MURDER," and the murder was stated to have been committed at South-green, near

Dartford, on the bodies of Thomas Lane, his wife, three children, and his mother. The murderer's conduct was stated very particularly, although, in fact, no such event occurred. The magistrate severely censured the conduct of the whole parties. He ordered the prisoners to be detained, and considered them to be very proper subjects to be made an example of. On Thursday these parties were again brought before the magistrate, together with Mrs. Catnach [the mother] the printer of the bills, which gave a fictitious statement of the horrid murder said to be committed at Dartford. She was severely reprimanded. The two hornblowers were also reprimanded and then discharged.

The busy year of 1820 was a very important one to Catnach, in fact the turning point in his life. The Duke of Kent, fourth son of George III., and father to Queen Victoria, died on the 23rd of January—the event was of sufficient consequence to produce several "Full Particulars," for street sale. Just six days after his death, viz., on the 29th of January, 1820, George III. died, and that event set the "Catnach Press" going night and day to supply the street papers, containing "Latest particulars," &c.

"Mourn, Britons mourn! Your sons deplore,
Our Royal Sovereign is now no more,"

was the commencement of a ballad written, printed, and published by J. Catnach, 2, Monmouth-court, 7 Dials. Battledores, Lotteries, and Primers sold cheap. Sold by Marshall, Bristol, and Hook, Brighton.

The royal body was committed to the family vault in St. George's Chapel at Windsor, on the 16th of February, amidst a concourse of the great and the noble of the land. The usual ceremony of proclamation and salutation announced the accession of George IV. and another important era commenced.

Immediately following these events came the Cato-street conspiracy. On the 24th of February the newspapers contained the startling intelligence that, on the previous evening, a party of eleven men, headed by Arthur Thistlewood, who was already known as a political agitator, had been apprehended at a stable in Cato-street, an obscure place in the locality of Grosvenor-square, on the charge of being the parties to a conspiracy to assassinate the greater part of the King's Ministers. The truth of the intelligence was soon confirmed by the proceedings which took place before the magisterial authorities; and in due course all the parties were put on their trial at the Old Bailey, on a charge of high treason, Arthur Thistlewood, the leader, being the first tried on the 17th of April; the Lord Chief Justice Abbott presiding. The names of the other prisoners were—William Davidson, a man of colour; James Ings, John Thomas Brunt, Richard Tidd, James William Wilson, John Harrison, Richard Bradburn, James Shaw Strange, and Charles Cooper, of whom the first four, together with Thistlewood, were executed as traitors on May 1st.

The Cato-street conspiracy proved a rich harvest to all concerned in the production of street literature. Catnach came in for a fair share of the work, and he found himself with plenty of cash in hand, and in good time to increase his trade-plant to meet the great demand for the street-papers that were in a few months to be published daily, and in reference to the ever-memorable trial of Queen Caroline; then it was that his business so enormously increased as at times to require three or four presses going night and day to keep pace with the great demand for papers, which contained a very much abridged account of the previous day's evidence, and taken without the least acknowledgment from an early procured copy of one of the daily newspapers.

Great as was the demand, the printers of street literature were equal to the occasion, and all were actively engaged in getting out "papers," squibs, lists of various trade deputations to the Queen's levées, lampoons and songs, that were almost hourly published, on the subject of the Queen's trial. The following is a selection from one which emanated from the "Catnach Press," and was supplied to us by John Morgan, the Seven Dials bard, and who added that he had the good luck—the times being prosperous—to screw out half-a-crown from Old Jemmy for the writing of it. "Ah! sir," he continued, "it was always a hard matter to get much out of Jemmy Catnach, I can tell you, sir. He was, at most times, a hard-fisted one, and no mistake about it. Yet, sir, somehow or another, he warn't such a bad sort, just where he took. A little bit rough and ready, like, you know, sir. But yet still a 'nipper.' That's just about the size of Jemmy Catnach, sir. I wish I could recollect more of the song, but you've got the marrow of it, sir:—

> ' And when the Queen arrived in town,
> The people called her good, sirs;
> She had a Brougham by her side,
> A Denman, and a Wood, sirs.
>
> ' The people all protected her,
> They ran from far and near, sirs,
> Till they reached the house of Squire Byng,
> Which was in St. James's-square, sirs.
>
> ' And there my blooming Caroline,
> About her made a fuss, man,
> And told how she had been deceived
> By a cruel, barbarous, husband ' "

Street papers continued to be printed and sold in connection with Queen Caroline's trial up to the date of her death, in the month of August, 1821.

A Copy of Verses in Praise of Queen Caroline.

"Ye Britons all, both great and small,
  Come listen to my ditty,
Your noble Queen, fair Caroline,
  Does well deserve your pity.

Like harmless lamb that sucks its dam,
  Amongst the flowery thyme,
Or turtle dove that's given to love:
  And that's her only crime.

Wedlock I ween, to her has been
  A life of grief and woe;
Thirteen years past she's had no rest,
  As Britons surely know.

> To blast her fame, men without shame,
>   Have done all they could do;
> 'Gainst her to swear they did prepare
>   A motley, perjured crew.
>
> Europe they seek for Turk or Greek,
>   To swear her life away,
> But she will triumph yet o'er all,
>   And innocence display.
>
> Ye powers above, who **virtue love**,
>   Protect her from despair,
> And soon her free from calumny,
>   Is every true man's prayer."

J. Catnach, Printer, 2, Monmouth Court, 7 Dials.

Immediately following the **Queen's death**, there were published a whole host of monodies, elegies, and ballads in her praise. Catnach made a great hit with **one** entitled—" Oh! Britons Remember your Queen's Happy Days," together with a large broadside, entitled "An Attempt to Exhibit the Leading Events in the Queen's Life, in Cuts and Verse. Adorned with Twelve splendid Illustrations. Interspersed with Verses of Descriptive Poetry. Entered at Stationers' Hall. By Jas. Catnach, Printer, 7 Dials. Price 2d." A copy is preserved in the British Museum. Press Mark. *Tab.* 597, *a*, 1—67, and arranged under CATNACH, from which we select two pieces as a fair sample of Jemmy's " poetry-making !"—Which please to read carefully, and " Mind Your Stops !" quoth John Berkshire.

An Elegy on the Death of the Queen.

CURS'D be the hour when on the British shore,
　　She set her foot—whose loss we now deplore;
For, from that hour she pass'd a life of woe,
And underwent what few could undergo:
And lest she should a tranquil hour know,
Against her peace was struck a deadly blow;
A separation hardly to be borne,—
Her only daughter from her arms was torn!
And next discarded—driven from her home,
An unprotected Wanderer to roam!
Oh, how each heart with indignation fills,
When memory glances o'er the train of ills,
Which through her travels followed everywhere
In quick succession till this fatal year!
Here let us stop—for mem'ry serves too well,
To bear the woes which Caroline befel,
Each art was tried—at last to crush her down,
The Queen of England was refus'd a crown!
Too much to bear—Thus robb'd of all her state
She fell a victim to their hate!
"They have destroy'd me,"—with her parting breath,
She died—and calmly yielded unto death.
Forgiving all, she parted with this life,
A Queen, and no Queen—wife, and not a wife!
To Heaven her soul is borne on Seraph's wings,
To wait the Judgment of the KING of Kings;
Trusting to find a better world than this,
And meet her Daughter in the realms of bliss.

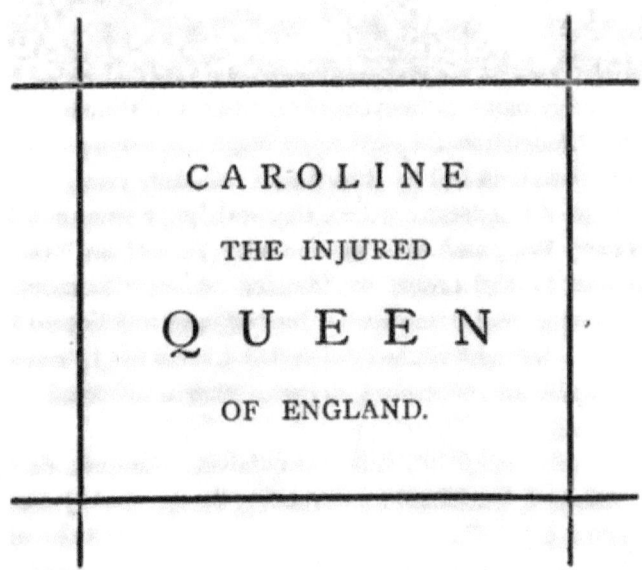

CAROLINE
THE INJURED
QUEEN
OF ENGLAND.

Beneath this cold marble the " Wanderer " lies,
    Here shall she rest 'till " the Heavens be no more,"
'Till the trumpet shall sound, and the Dead shall arise,
    Then the perjurer unmask'd will his sentence deplore.
Ah! what will avail then? Pomp, Titles, and Birth,
    Those empty distinctions all levell'd will be,
For the King shall be judg'd with the poor of the earth,
    And perhaps, the poor man will be greater than he.
Until that day we leave Caroline's wrongs,
    Meantime, may " Repentance " her foes overtake ;
O grant it, kind POWER, to whom alone it belongs.
    AMEN. Here an end of this Hist'ry we make.

       Quod. JAS. C-T-N-H, Dec. 10th, 1821.

In the early part of the year 1821, the British public were informed through the then existing usual advertising mediums that there was about to be published, in monthly parts, " Pierce Egan's Life in London ; or, the Day and Night Scenes of Jerry Hawthorn, Esq., and his elegant friend Corinthian Tom, accompanied by Bob Logic, the Oxonian, in their Rambles and Sprees through the Metropolis. Embellished with Scenes from Real Life, designed and etched by I. R. and G. Cruikshank, and enriched with numerous original designs on wood by the same Artists."

And on the 15th of July, the first number, price one shilling, was published by Messrs. Sherwood, Neely, and Jones, of Paternoster Row. This sample, or first instalment, of the entire work was quite enough for society to judge by. It took both town and country by storm. It was found to be the exact thing in literature that the readers of those days wanted. Edition after edition was called for—and supplied, as fast as the illustrations could be got away from the small army of women and children who were colouring them. With the appearance of numbers two and three, the demand increased, and a revolution in our literature, in our drama, and even in our nomenclature began to develope itself. All the announcements from Paternoster Row were of books, great and small, depicting life in London ; dramatists at once turned their attention to the same subject, and tailors, bootmakers, and hatters, recommended nothing but Corinthian shapes, and Tom and Jerry patterns.*

---

* The late John Camden Hotten's Introduction to the new edition of "Life in London." Chatto & Windus: Piccadilly.

TOM AND JERRY.

> "Of Life in London, Tom, Jerry and Logic I sing."
> To the Strand then I toddled—the mob was great—
> My watch I found gone—pockets undone:
> I fretted at first, and rail'd against fate,
> For I paid well to see "LIFE IN LONDON."

As may be readily conceived; the stage soon claimed "Tom and Jerry." The first drama founded upon the work was from the pen of Mr. Barrymore, and produced—"in hot haste," at the Royal Amphitheatre, on Monday, Sept. 17, 1821. The second dramatic version was written for the Olympic Theatre, by Charles Dibden, and first played on Monday, Nov. 12, 1821.

Mr. Moncrieff appeared as the third on the list of dramatists, and it was announced at the Adelphi Theatre in the following style:—"On Monday, Nov. 26th, 1821, will be presented for the first time, on a scale of unprecedented extent (having been many weeks in preparation under the superintendence of several of the most celebrated Artists, both in the *Ups and Downs* of Life, who have all kindly come forward to assist the Proprietors in their endeavours to render the Piece a complete out-and-outer), an entirely new Classic, Comic, Operatic, Didactic, Aristophanic, Localic, Analytic, Panoramic, Camera-

Obscura-ic Extravaganza-Burletta of Fun, Frolic, Fashion and Flash, in three acts, called 'TOM and JERRY; or LIFE in LONDON.' Replete with Prime Chaunts, Rum Glees, and Kiddy Catches, founded on Pierce Egan's well-known and highly popular work of the same name, by a celebrated extravagant erratic Author. The music selected and modified by him from the most eminent composers, ancient and modern, and every Air furnished with an attendant train of Graces. The costumes and scenery superintended by Mr. I. R. Cruikshank, from the Drawings by himself and his brother, Mr. George Cruikshank, the celebrated Artists of the original Work.

"Corinthian Tom, Mr. Wrench; Jerry Hawthorn, Mr. John Reeve; Logic, Mr. Wilkinson; Jemmy Green, Mr. Keeley; Dusty Bob, Mr. Walbourn; African Sal, Mr. Sanders; Billy Waters, Mr. Paulo; Kate, Mrs. Baker; Sue, Mrs. Waylett, &c., &c.

BLACK SAL AND DUSTY BOB.

Besides the authors already mentioned, Tom Dibden, Farrell, and Douglas Jerrold, each produced dramas upon the popular theme, and during the seasons of 1821-2, "Life in London" was performed with *éclat*, at ten theatres in and around the metropolis, to overflowing houses. But Pierce Egan at length became tired of the successes of the playwrights in using his book, and resolved to try his own hand at a dramatic version— or, as he termed it, to "take a leaf out of his own book,"— and the AUTHOR'S PIECE was "got up" and performed for the first time at Sadler's Wells, under the management of Mr. Egerton, on Monday, April 8, 1822, with most decided success.

It was thus announced by Mrs. Egerton, in the address written for the occasion by T. Greenwood, Esq. :—

> "To-night my friends, this modern taste to meet,
> We show you JERRY at his country seat :
> Then up to town transport the rustic beau,
> And show him 'Life in London,' HIGH and LOW."

At length TOM and JERRY had been repeated so often in the Metropolis, that the performers, notwithstanding the great applause they nightly received in the above piece, absolutely became tired and worn-out with the repetition of their characters, when the following piece of satire, written by T. Greenwood, Esq., was published, entitled, "The Tears of Pierce Egan, Esq., for the Death of 'Life in London ;' or, the Funeral of Tom and Jerry, dedicated to Robert and George Cruikshank, Esqs. Price Two Shillings, with an engraving by George Cruikshank."

> "Beat out of the Pit and thrown over the Ropes,
> TOM and JERRY resign'd their last breath,
> With them, too, expired the Managers' hopes,
> Who are left to deplore their sad death !

" Odd and various reports of the cause are about,
   But the real one was *this*, I opine :
They were run to a *standstill*, and, therefore, no doubt,
   That the cause was a rapid *decline*.

" When Death showed his *Nob*, out of *Time* they were beat,
   And neither would come to the *scratch* ;
They hung down their heads and gave up the last heat,
   Not prepared with the Spectre to *match*.

" All wept at the FUNERAL ! the FANCY and all—
   Some new, but a great many mended :
And EGAN, while CRUIKSHANK and *Bob* held the pall,
   As *Chief-Mourner* in person attended ! ! !

"Their *Sprees* and their *Rambles* no more shall amuse,
   Farewell to all nocturnal parleys ;
The Town felt regret as the bell tolled the news,
   And no one rejoiced—but the *Charleys !*

"A monument, too, their kind Patrons will raise,
   Inscribed on—' Here lies TOM and JERRY,
Who, departing the *stage* to their immortal praise,
   ONE THOUSAND NIGHTS made the *Town Merry ! ! !* '

" May their souls rest in peace, since they've chosen to flit,
   Like other great heroes departed ;
May no mischief arise from the *sudden* exit,
   Nor PIERCE EGAN die—*broken-hearted !* "

In reference to the above, Pierce Egan states in "The Finish to the Adventures of Tom, Jerry, and Logic," that Catnach, in less than twelve hours after the publication, produced a pirated edition for street sale, for twopence.

Mr. Pierce Egan, in his " *Finish*," states that he reckoned no less than sixty-five separate publications, which he enumerates *in extenso*, all derived from his own work, and adds, with his usual amount of large and small CAPITALS and *italics*—" We have been *pirated*, COPIED, *traduced*; but unfortunately, not ENRICHED by our indefatigable exertions; therefore NOTORIETY must satisfy us, instead of the smiles of FORTUNE."

Jemmy Catnach, true to his line of life, soon joined what Pierce Egan designates as the "Mob of Literary Pirates," and brought out a "whole sheet" for street-sale, entitled "Life in London," with twelve woodcuts, which are reduced and very roughly executed copies of the centre figures of the original plates by the Brothers Cruikshank—but all in reverse. The letter-press matter consists of a poetical epitome of the plot and design of the original work of " Life in London." And taking it as it stands, and from whence it emanated, rather a creditable performance, particularly when we take into consideration—as duly announced by the street-patterer, that it was "Just printed and pub—lish—ed, all for the low charge of twopence."

On the rarity of this Catnachian and pirated edition of "Life in London" it is superfluous to enlarge, and it is easy to account for this circumstance, if we reflect that the broadside form of publication is by no means calculated for preservation; hundreds of similar pieces printed for street-sale must have perished. The more generally acceptable a broadside or street ballad became, and was handed about for perusal, the more it was exposed to the danger of destruction. No copy of Catnach's version is preserved in the British Museum, therefore, and for the reason above stated, it must be considered as a great "Literary Rarity."*

---

* Our thanks are due, and are hereby given to Mr. Crawford John Pocock, of Cannon Place, Brighton, for the loan and use of his—what we feel almost inclined to consider—unique copy of Catnach's broadside of "Life in London."

CUT I.—JERRY IN TRAINING FOR A SWELL.

NOW Jerry must needs be a swell,
    His coat must have a swallow-tail,
And Mr. Snip, so handy, O,
Soon rigg'd him out a Dandy, O.

CUT II.—TOM AND JERRY AMONG THE LADIES.

LADIES, your most humble servants,
    Tom and Jerry stand before you.
Our blood is thrilling, you're so killing;
At once we love you and adore you.

CUT III.—Jerry Loses at Play.

A T St. James's they dine, when, flushed with new wine,
    To the Gaming Tables they reel,
Where blacklegs and sharps, often gammon the flats,
    As their pockets do presently feel.

CUT IV.—Jerry Learning to Spar.

N OW Jerry's become a Fancy blade,
    To Jackson's he often goes,
And to shew his skill in the milling trade,
    He crack'd poor Logick's nose.

CUT V.—Tom and Jerry at a Fortune-Teller's.

HERE lives a Fortune-Telling Gipsy,
　　Wrinkled, crabbed, grim and old;
And Tom and Jerry's fancy ladies
　　Are gone to get their Fortunes told.

CUT VI.—Beggar's Opera. Tom, Jerry, and Logick among the Cadgers in the Holy Land.

NOW to keep up the spree, Tom, Jerry and Logick,
　　Went disguis'd to the Slums in the Holy Land;
Through each crib and each court, they hunted for sport,
　　Till they came to the Beggar's Opera so named.

CUT VII.—NIGHT SCENE.—TOM AND JERRY UPSETTING THE CHARLEYS.

HARK! the watchman springs his rattle,
    Now the midnight lark's begun;
Boxes crashing, lanthorns smashing,
    Mill the Charleys—oh! what fun.

CUT VIII.—BROUGHT BEFORE THE MAGISTRATES.

AN' please your Worship here's three fellows
    Been hammering of us all about;
Broke our boxes, lanthorns, smellers,
    And almost clos'd our peepers up.

CUT IX.—Tom, Jerry, and Logick in a Row.

Mercy! what a din and clatter
 Breaks the stillness of the night,
Lamps do rattle—'tis a battle,
 Quick, and let us see the sight.

CUT X.—Scene in a Gin-shop.

Here some are tumbling and jumping in,
 And some are staggering out;
One's pawn'd her smock for a quartern of gin,
 Another, her husband's coat.

CUT XI.—POOR LOGICK IN THE FLEET.

ALL in the Fleet poor Logick's moor'd
His swaggering's now at an end!

CUT XII.—JERRY GOING BACK TO THE COUNTRY.

THREE merry boys were Logick, Tom and Jerry,
And many funny larks they have seen;
Farewell, gay London, the country calls me home again,
The coach moves on—the play is done—Goodbye, Goodbye.

Quod. JAS. C-N-H, March 23, 1822.

How delightful Pierce Egan's book was to the youths of England, and how eagerly all its promised feasts of pleasure were devoured by them, Thackeray has told us in his "Roundabout Papers—DE JUVENTUTE" in the "Cornhill Magazine" for October, 1860.

Mr., afterwards Sir William Cubitt, of Ipswich, erected a treadmill at Brixton Gaol, and soon afterwards in other large prisons. A street ballad on the subject was issued from the "Catnach Press" and had a most unprecedented sale, keeping the pressmen and boys working for weeks—

"And we're all treading at fam'd Brixton Mill."

The treadmill—that "terror to evil doers"—excited much attention, and the inventor's name gave rise to many jokes on the subject among such of the prisoners as could laugh at their own crimes, who said they were punished by the *cubit!*.

THE TREADMILL.

THIS Brixton Mill's a fearful ill,
   And he who brought the Bill in,
Is threat'n'd by the *cribbing* coves,
   That he shall have a *milling*.
They say he shew'd a simple pate,
   To think of felons mending;
As every *step* which here they take
   They're still in crime *ascending*.

Tom, Jerry, Logic, three prime sprigs,
   Find here they cannot *come* it,
For though their *fancy* soars aloft,
   They ne'er will reach the *summit*.
Corinthian Kate and buxom Sue
   Must change their *warm* direction,
For if they make one *false step* more
   They'll have *Cold Bath Correction*.

"The gallows does well: But how does it well? it does well to those that do ill."—*Hamlet*, Act v., sc. i.

There can be little doubt that Jemmy Catnach, the great publisher of the Seven Dials, had his mind mostly centred upon the chronicling of doubtful scandals, fabulous duels between ladies of fashion, "cooked" assassinations, and sudden deaths of eminent individuals, apochryphal elopements, real or catchpenny account of murders, impossible robberies, delusive suicides, dark deeds, and—though last, not least, in *his* love—public executions, *vulgo* "Hanging Matches," to which was usually attached the all-important and necessary "Sorrowful Lamentations," or "Copy of Affectionate Verses," which according to the established custom, the criminal composed in the condemned cell the night before his execution, after this manner:—

THE HISTORY OF

The Flying Stationer, otherwise Patterer.

"All you that have got feeling, I pray you now attend
To these few lines so sad and true, a solemn silence lend;
It is of a cruel murder, to you I will unfold——
The bare recital of the tale must make your blood run cold."

"Mercy on earth I'll not implore, to crave it would be vain,
My hands are dyed with human gore, none can wash off the stain,
But the merits of a Saviour, whose mercy alone I crave;
Good Christians pray, as thus I die, I may His pardon have."

A mournful and affecting COPY OF VERSES on the death of ANN WILLIAMS,

Who was barbarously and cruelly murdered by her sweetheart, W. JONES, near Wirksworth, in Derbyshire, July, 1823.

William Jones, a young man aged 20, has been fully committed to Derby gaol for the murder of his sweetheart, under circumstances of unheard of barbarity. The poor victim was a servant girl, whose under pretence of marriage he seduced. On her proving with child the villain formed the horrid design of murdering her, and carried his diabolical plan into execution on Monday evening last. The following verses are written upon the occasion, giving a complete detail of this shocking affair:—

Come all false hearted young men
   And listen to my song,
'Tis of a cruel murder,
   That lately has been done
On the body of a maiden fair
   The truth I will unfold,
The bare relation of this deed
   Will make your blood run cold.
Near Wirksworth town in Derbyshire,
   Ann Williams she did dwell,
In service she long time had lived,
   Till this to her befel.
Her cheeks were like the blushing rose
   All in the month of May,
Which made this wicked young man
   Thus unto her did say:
Nancy, my charming creature,
   You have my heart ensnared,
My love is such I am resolved
   To wed you I declare.
Thus by his false deluding tongue
   Poor Nancy was beguil'd,
And soon to her misfortune,
   By him she proved with child.
Some days ago this damsel fair
   Did write to him with speed,
Such tenderness she did express
   Would make a heart to bleed.
She said, my dearest William,
   I am with child by thee,
Therefore, my dear, pray let me know
   When you will marry me.
The following day at evening,
   This young man did repair,
Unto the town of Wirksworth,
   To meet his Nancy there.
Saying, Nancy dear, come let us walk,
   Among the flowery fields,
And then the secrets of my heart
   To you I will reveal.
O then this wicked young man
   A knife he did provide,
And all unknown to his true love
   Concealed it by his side.
When to the fatal spot they came,

These words to her did say:
All on this very night I will
   Your precious life betray.
On bended knees she then did fall,
   In sorrow and despair,
Aloud for mercy she did call,
   Her cries did rend the air;
With clasped hands and uplift eyes
   She cried, Oh spare my life,
I never more will ask you
   To make me your wedded wife.
O then this wicked young man said,
   No mercy will I show;
He took the knife all from his side,
   And pierced her body through.
But still she smiling said to him,
   While trembling with fear,
Ah! William, William, spare my life,
   Think on your baby dear.
Twice more then with the bloody knife
   He ran her body through,
Her throat was cut from ear to ear,
   Most dreadful for to view;
Her hands and arms and beauteous face
   He cut and mangled sore,
While down upon her milk white breast
   The crimson blood did pour.
He took the shawl from off her neck,
   And round her body tied,
With pebble stones he did it fill,
   Thinking the crime to hide.
O then into the silver stream
   He plunged her straightway,
But with her precious blood was stained,
   Which soon did him betray.
O then this young man taken was,
   And into prison sent,
In rattling chains he is confin'd,
   His crime for to lament,
Until the Assizes do come on,
   When trembling he must stand,
Reflecting on the deed he's done;
   Waiting the dread command.
Now all you thoughtless young men
   A timely warning take;
Likewise ye fair young maidens,
   For this poor damsel's sake.
And Oh beware of flattering tongues,
   For they'll your ruin prove;
So may his crown your future day,
   In comfort, joy, and love.

Or take another and stereotyped example, which from time to time has served equally well for the verses *written by* the culprit—Brown, Jones, Robinson, or Smith :

> "Those deeds I mournfully repent,
>   But now it is too late,
> The day is past, the die is cast,
>   And fixed is my fate.
>
> "I see the hangman before me stand,
>   Ready to seize me by the law's command ;
> When my life is ended on the fatal tree,
>   Then will be clear'd up all mystery."

Occasionally the Last Sorrowful Lamentation contained a "Love Letter"—the criminal being unable, in some instances, to read or write, being no obstacle to the composition—written according to the street patterer's statement: "from the depths of the condemned cell, with the condemned pen, ink, and paper." This mode of procedure in "gallows" literature, and this style of composition having prevailed for from sixty to seventy years.

Then they would say : "Here you have also an exact likeness of the murderer, taken at the bar of the Old Bailey by an eminent artist !" when all the time it was an old woodcut that had been used for every criminal for many years. The *block !* opposite, to our own knowledge, served as the *counterfeit* presentment of all popular murderers for upwards of forty years.

LIKENESS OF THE MURDERER.

"There's nothing beats a stunning good murder after all," said a "running patterer" to Mr. Henry Mayhew, the author of "London Labour and London Poor." It is only fair to assume that Mr. James Catnach shared in the sentiment, for it is said that he made over £500 by the publication of:—

"The Full, True and Particular Account of the Murder of Mr. Weare by John Thurtell and his Companions, which took place on the 24th of October, 1823, in Gill's Hill-lane, near Elstree, in Hertfordshire:—Only One Penny."

There were eight formes set up, for old Jemmy had no notion of stereotyping in those days, and pressmen had to re-cover their own tympans with sheep-skins. But by working day and night for a week they managed to get off about 250,000 copies with the four presses, each working two formes at a time.

THURTELL MURDERING MR. WEARE.

As the trial progressed, and the case became more fully developed, the public mind became almost insatiable. Every night and morning large bundles were despatched to the principal towns in the three kingdoms.

One of the many street-ballads on the subject informed the British public that :—

"Thurtell, Hunt, and Probert, too, for trial must now prepare,
For that horrid murder of Mr. William Weare."

The circumstances immediately attending the murder are so fully and so well detailed in the proper channels that we need not here say more than that the trial took place at Hertford on the 5th January, 1824.

The prisoners who stood indicted were John Thurtell and Joseph Hunt. The latter was at the time well known as a public singer and was somewhat celebrated for the talent which he possessed. Both prisoners were found guilty, but Hunt was reprieved and subsequently ordered to be transported for life. Thurtell, who fully confessed to the crime, was executed in front of Hertford gaol on Friday, the 9th of January, 1824.

As before observed, Catnach cleared over £500 by this event, and was so loth to leave it, that when a wag put him up to a joke, and showed him how he might set the thing a-going again, he could not withstand it; and so, about a fortnight after Thurtell had been hanged, Jemmy brought out a startling broad-sheet, headed, "WE ARE ALIVE AGAIN!" He put so little space between the words "WE" and "ARE" that it looked at first sight like "WEARE." Many thousands were bought by the ignorant and gullible public, but those who did not like the trick called it a "catch penny," and this gave rise to this peculiar term, which ever afterwards stuck to the issues of the "Seven Dials' Press," though they sold as well as ever.

Probert, who had been mixed up in the affair, was admitted as King's evidence and discharged at the rising of the Court. He subsequently met the fate he so richly deserved, for, having been found guilty at the Old Bailey of horse stealing, he was executed there on the 20th of June, 1825.

THE CONFESSION AND EXECUTION OF
JOHN THURTELL
AT HERTFORD GAOL,
On Friday, the 9th of January, 1824.

THE EXECUTION.
Hertford, half-past twelve o'clock.

This morning, at ten minutes before twelve, a bustle among the javelin-men stationed within the boarded enclosure on which the drop was erected, announced to the multitude without that the preparations for the execution were nearly concluded. The javelin-men proceeded to arrange themselves in the order usually observed upon these melancholy but necessary occurrences. They had scarcely finished their arrangements, when the opening of the gate of the prison gave an additional impulse to public anxiety.

When the clock was on the stroke of twelve, Mr Nicholson, the Under-Sheriff, and the executioner ascended the platform, followed on to it by Thurtell, who mounted the stairs with a slow but steady step. The principal turnkey of the gaol came next, and was followed by Mr Wilson and two officers. On the approach of the prisoner being intimated by those persons who, being in an elevated situation, obtained the first view of him, all the immense multitude present took off their hats.

Thurtell immediately placed himself under the fatal beam, and at that moment the chimes of a neighbouring clock began to strike twelve. The executioner then came forward with the rope, which he threw across it. Thurtell first lifted his eyes up to the drop, gazed at it for a few moments, and then took a calm but hurried survey of the multitude around him. He next fixed his eyes on a young gentleman in the crowd, whom he had frequently seen as a spectator at the commencement of the proceedings against him. Seeing that the individual was affected by the circumstance, he removed them to another quarter, and in so doing recognised an individual well known in the sporting circles, to whom he made a slight bow.

The prisoner was attired in a dark brown great coat, with a black velvet collar, white corduroy breeches, drab gaiters and shoes. His hands were confined with handcuffs, instead of being tied with cord, as is usually the case on such occasions, and, at his own request, his arms were not pinioned. He wore a pair of black kid gloves, and the wrists of his shirt were visible below the cuffs of his coat. As on the last day of his trial, he wore a white cravat. The irons, which were very heavy, and consisted of a succession of chain links, were still on his legs, and were held up in the middle by a Belcher handkerchief tied round his waist.

The executioner commenced his mournful duties by taking from the unhappy prisoner his cravat and collar. To obviate all difficulty in this stage of the proceedings, Thurtell flung back his head and neck, and so gave the executioner an opportunity of immediately divesting him of that part of his dress. After tying the rope round Thurtell's neck, the executioner drew a white cotton cap over his countenance, which did not, however, conceal the contour of his face, or deprive him entirely of the view of surrounding objects.

At that moment the clock sounded the last stroke of twelve. During the whole of this appalling ceremony, there was not the slightest symptom of emotion discernible in his features; his demeanour was perfectly calm and tranquil, and he behaved like a man acquainted with the dreadful ordeal he was about to pass, but not unprepared to meet it. Though his fortitude was thus conspicuous, it was evident from his appearance that in the interval between his conviction and his execution he must have suffered much. He looked careworn; his countenance had assumed a cadaverous hue, and there was a haggardness and lankness about his cheeks and mouth, which could not fail to attract the notice of every spectator.

The executioner next proceeded to adjust the noose by which Thurtell was to be attached to the scaffold. After he had fastened it in such a manner as to satisfy his own mind, Thurtell looked up at it, and examined it with great attention. He then desired the executioner to let him have fall enough. The rope at this moment seemed as if it would only give a fall of two or three feet. The executioner assured him that the fall was quite sufficient. The principal turnkey then went up to Thurtell, shook hands with him, and turned away in tears. Mr Wilson, the governor of the gaol, next approached him. Thurtell said to him, "Do you think, Mr Wilson, I have got enough fall?" Mr Wilson replied, "I think you have, sir. Yes, quite enough." Mr Wilson then took hold of his hand, shook it, and said, "Good bye, Mr Thurtell, may God Almighty bless you." Thurtell instantly replied, "God bless you, Mr Wilson, God bless you." Mr Wilson next asked him whether he considered that the laws of his country had been dealt to him justly and fairly, upon which he said, "I admit that justice has been done me—I am perfectly satisfied."

A few seconds then elapsed, during which every person seemed to be engaged in examining narrowly Thurtell's deportment. His features, as well as they could be discerned, appeared to remain unmoved, and his hands, which were extremely prominent, continued perfectly steady, and were not affected by the slightest tremulous motion.

Exactly at two minutes past twelve the Under-Sheriff, with his wand, gave the dreadful signal—the drop suddenly and silently fell—and

JOHN THURTELL WAS LAUNCHED
INTO ETERNITY.

On the 10th of September, 1824, Henry Fauntleroy, of the firm of Marsh, Stracey, Fauntleroy, and Graham, bankers, in Berners-street, was apprehended in consequence of its being discovered that in September, 1820, £10,000 3 per cent. stock, standing in the names of himself, J. D. Hume, and John Goodchild, as trustees of Francis William Bellis, had been sold out under a power of attorney, to which the names of his co-trustees and some of the subscribing witnesses were forged. It was soon ascertained that the extent to which this practice had been carried was enormous, no less than £170,000 stock having been sold out in 1814 and 1815 by the same fraudulent means.

Every exertion was used by Mr. Fauntleroy's counsel, his case being twice argued before the Judges, but both decisions were against him; and on the 30th of November, 1824, his execution took place. The number of persons assembled was estimated at nearly 100,000.

The station in society of this unfortunate man, and the long-established respectability of the banking-house, in which he was the most active partner, with the vast extent of the forgeries committed, gave to his case an intensity of interest which has scarcely ever been equalled, and during the whole time it was pending afforded plenty of work for the printers and vendors of street literature. Catnach's advanced position, which was now far beyond all his compeers, caused him to get the lion's share. Every incident in the man's character, history, and actions was taken advantage of. The sheets, almost wet from the press, were read by high and low; by those who lived and revelled in marble halls and gilded saloons, as well as by those who thronged our large towns and centres of industry.

The parliamentary election of 1826, for the county of Northumberland, the principal seat of which was at Alnwick, gave early promise of being severely contested. There were four candidates in the field, namely, Henry Thomas Liddell, afterwards first Earl of Ravensworth, of Ravensworth Castle, county Durham; Mr. Matthew Bell, of Woolsingham, Northumberland; Mr. Thomas Wentworth Beaumont, and Lord Howick, afterwards Henry the third Earl Grey, K.G. The nomination of the candidates took place on Tuesday, June 20th, 1826, and the polling continued till July 6th, when the result was as follows:—

Liddell	1562
Bell	1380
Beaumont	1335
Howick	997

This contest was the greatest political event in the history of the county. It is estimated that it cost the candidates little short of £250,000.

Now, as we have before observed, Mr. Mark Smith—who till the time of his death, on the 18th of May, 1881, aged 87—carried on the business of printer and bookseller at Alnwick—and James Catnach, were fellow apprentices, both being bound to learn the art of printing to the elder Catnach on the same day. This early-formed acquaintanceship continued throughout the remaining portion of Catnach's life, and whenever Mr. Mark Smith came to London in after years, he always visited Jemmy's house.

It was in consequence of the continued friendship existing between Mr. Mark Smith and Jemmy Catnach that the latter had often expressed a desire to serve his fellow-apprentice, should circumstances occur to render it necessary. The Alnwick election of 1826 promised to be a good one as regarded printing, and Mr. Smith anticipating a difficulty in getting through his work, applied to Catnach to know if he could render him any assistance. The result was that Jemmy at once proffered to go to Alnwick and take with him a small hand-press. After his arrival he seldom went out of the house, as all hands worked early and late, for, besides addresses, squibs, &c., they had to get out the state of the poll every afternoon, shortly after four o'clock. The number of addresses and squibs, in prose and verse, during this memorable election was enormous. The whole, when collected together, forms four good-sized volumes. The principal printers in Alnwick at this time, and who were engaged by the candidates, were Smith, Davison, and Graham. But there was a great deal of printing done at Newcastle, Gateshead, North Shields, Morpeth, and other towns.

There can be but little doubt that all who were professionally engaged at this election made a good thing out of it. The money spent upon printing alone must have been very great. And nearly all the public-houses in Alnwick were made "open houses," as well as most of those in the principal towns throughout the county. Old people talk to this day, with a degree of pride of "those good old times" that existed at the Parliamentary elections previous to the passing of the Reform Bill of 1832. As far as Catnach was concerned, he merely went to help to pay off a deep debt of gratitude owing by him to the Smith family for many past favours to his own family when they were in, dire distress in *auld lang syne*. Besides, Jemmy was now getting towards that state known as being "comfortably well-to-do," and the trip was a change of air—a bit of a holiday, and a visit to the town of his birth. And as he had buried his mother in London during the early part of the year, he took the opportunity to erect in the parish churchyard, that which at once stands as a cenotaph and a tombstone, bearing the following inscription :—

>"JOHN, Son of JOHN CATNACH,
>Printer, died August 27th,
>1794, Aged 5 years & 7 months.
>JOHN CATNACH died in
>LONDON, 1813, Aged 44.
>MARY, his wife died Jany.
>24th, 1826, Aged 60 years,
>Also John, Margaret, and
>Jane Catnach, lie here." *

During Catnach's absence from London on the Alnwick election, his old rivals—the Pitts family—were, as usual, concocting false reports, and exhibiting lampoons, after the following manner :—

>"Poor Jemmy with the son of Old Nick,
>Down to Northumberland he's gone ;
>To take up his freedom at Alnwick,
>The why or the wherefore's known to none.

>"Before he went, he washed in soap and sud,
>The Alnwick folks they found the fiddle ;
>Then they dragged poor Jemmy through the mud,
>Two foot above his middle.

The above was in allusion to the old ceremony of being dragged through the dirty pool to be made a Freeman of the town of Alnwick. But, as far as Catnach was concerned, there is no truth whatever in the matter, it was simply "a weak invention of the enemy." It was in the latter part of June and the beginning of July in the same year, that Catnach was at Alnwick, and the ceremony of making freemen always took place on St. Mark's Day, April 25th, or at least two months earlier.

---

* The above copied, *verbatim* At our request, by Mr. George Skelly, of Alnwick.

Thus the statement of the Pitts' party was—

> "As false
> As air, as water, as wind, as sandy earth,
> As fox to lamb, as wolf to heifer's calf,
> Pard to the hind, or step-dame to her son."

Catnach, as the high priest of the literature of the streets, surrounded by trade rivals, "stood like a man at a mark with a whole army shooting at him," but he was as firm as a rock and with the strength of a giant, and, as Hyperion to a Satyr, defied them all.

The destruction of the Royal Brunswick Theatre, Well-street, Wellclose-square, East London, on the 29th of February, 1828, by the falling in of the walls, in consequence of too much weight being attached to the heavy cast-iron roof, made a rare nine-day's wonder for the workers of street-papers. Fortunately the catastrophe happened in the day-time, during the rehearsal of "Guy Mannering," and only fifteen persons perished, viz :—

Mr. D. S. Maurice, a master printer, of Fenchurch-street, one of the Proprietors,

Mr. J. Evans	... *Bristol Observer*	Mr. J. Purdy	... *Blacksmith*,
Miss Mary A. Feron	... *Actress*,	Messrs. J. Miles, W. Leader, A. W. Davidson, M. Miles, and J. Abbott ... ... *Carpenters*,	
Miss Freeman	... *Corps de ballet*,		
Mr. E. Gilbert	... *Comedian*,		
Mr. J. Blamire	... *Property Man*,	J. Levy, *A Clothesman* (accidentally passing).	
Mr. G. Penfold	... *Doorkeeper*,		
Miss Jane Wall	... *Visitor*,		

"Oh yes, sir ! I remember well the falling of the Brunswick Theatre, out Whitechapel way. It was a rare good thing for all the running and standing patterers in and about ten miles of London. Every day we all killed more and more people—in our "Latest Particulars." One day there was twenty persons killed, the next day thirty or forty, until it got at last to be worked up to about a hundred, and all killed. Then we killed all sorts of people, Duke of Wellington, and all the Dukes and Duchesses, Bishops, swell nobs and snobs we could think of at the moment."

ATROCIOUS MURDER OF A YOUNG WOMAN IN SUFFOLK.

SINGULAR DISCOVERY OF THE BODY FROM A DREAM.

THE RED BARN.

THE SCENE OF THE MURDER, AND WHERE THE BODY OF MARIA MARTEN WAS FOUND CONCEALED.

Four years after the Thurtell and Weare affair, namely, in the month of April, 1828, another "sensational" murder was discovered—that of Maria Marten, by William Corder, in the Red Barn, at Polstead, in the county of Suffolk. The circumstances that led to the discovery of this most atrocious murder, were of an extraordinary and romantic nature, and manifest an almost special interposition of Providence in marking out the offender. As the mother of the girl had on three several nights dreamt that her daughter was murdered and buried in Corder's Red Barn, and as this proved to be the case, an additional "charm" was given to the circumstance. The "Catnach Press" was again set working both day and night, to meet the great demand for the "Full Particulars." In due course came the gratifying announcement of the apprehension of the murderer! and the sale continued unabatingly in both town and country, every "Flying Stationer" making great profits by the sale.

LIKENESS OF WILLIAM CORDER.

The trial of Corder took place at Bury St. Edmonds, on the 7th of August, 1828, before the Lord Chief Baron (Anderson). The prisoner pleaded "*Not Guilty*," and the trial proceeded. On being called on for his defence, Corder read a manuscript paper. He declared that he deeply deplored the death of the unfortunate deceased, and he urged the jury to dismiss from their minds all that prejudice which must necessarily have been excited against him by the public press, &c. Having concluded his address, the Lord Chief Baron summed up, and a verdict of "*Guilty*" was returned. The Last Dying Speech and Confession had an enormous sale—estimated at 1,166,000, a *facsimile* copy of which with the "Lamentable Verses," said to have been written by Old Jemmy Catnach will be found on the next page

CONFESSION AND EXECUTION OF
WILLIAM CORDER,
THE MURDERER OF MARIA MARTEN.

Since the tragical affair between Thurtell and Weare, no event has occurred connected with the criminal annals of our country which has excited so much interest as the trial of Corder, who was justly convicted of the murder of Maria Marten on Friday last.

THE CONFESSION.

"*Bury Gaol*, August 10th, 1828.—Condemned cell "Sunday evening, half-past Eleven.

"I acknowledge being guilty of the death of poor Maria Marten, by shooting her with a pistol. The particulars are as follows:—When we left her father's house, we began quarrelling about the burial of the child: she apprehended the place wherein it was deposited would be found out. The quarrel continued about three quarters of an hour upon this sad and about other subjects. A scuffle ensued, and during the scuffle, and at the time I think that she had hold of me, I took the pistol from the side pocket of my velveteen jacket and fired. She fell, and died in an instant. I never saw her even struggle. I was overwhelmed with agitation and dismay:—the body fell near the front doors on the floor of the barn. A vast quantity of blood issued from the wound, and ran on to the floor and through the crevices. Having determined to bury the body in the barn (about two hours after she was dead. I went and borrowed a spade of Mrs Stow, but before I went there I dragged the body from the barn into the chaff-house, and locked the barn. I returned again to the barn, and began to dig a hole, but the spade being a bad one, and the earth firm and hard, I was obliged to go home for a pickaxe and a better spade, with which I dug the hole, and then buried the body. I think I dragged the body by the handkerchief that was tied round her neck. It was dark when I finished covering up the body. I went the next day, and washed the blood from off the barn-floor. I declare to Almighty God I had no sharp instrument about me, and no other wound but the one made by the pistol was inflicted by me. I have been guilty of great idleness, and at times led a dissolute life, but I hope through the mercy of God to be forgiven. WILLIAM CORDER."

Witness to the signing by the said William Corder,
JOHN ORRIDGE.

Condemned cell, Eleven o'clock, Monday morning, August 11th, 1828.

The above confession was read over carefully to the prisoner in our presence, who stated most solemnly it was true, and that he had nothing to add to or retract from it.—W. STOCKING, chaplain ; TIMOTHY R. HOLMES, Under-Sheriff.

THE EXECUTION.

At ten minutes before twelve o'clock the prisoner was brought from his cell and pinioned by the hangman, who was brought from London for the purpose. He appeared resigned, but was so weak as to be unable to stand without support; when his cravat was removed he groaned heavily, and appeared to be labouring under great mental agony. When his wrists and arms were made fast, he was led round towards the scaffold, and as he passed the different yards in which the prisoners were confined, he shook hands with them, and speaking to two of them by name, he said, "Good bye, God bless you." They appeared considerably affected by the wretched appearance which he made, and "God bless you!" "May God receive your soul!" were frequently uttered as he passed along. The chaplain walked before the prisoner, reading the usual Burial Service, and the Governor and Officers walking immediately after him. The prisoner was supported to the steps which led to the scaffold; he looked somewhat wildly around, and a constable was obliged to support him while the hangman was adjusting the fatal cord. There was a barrier to keep off the crowd, amounting to upwards of 7,000 persons, who at this time had stationed themselves in the adjoining fields, on the hedges, the tops of houses, and at every point from which a view of the execution could be best obtained. The prisoner, a few moments before the drop fell, groaned heavily, and would have fallen, had not a second constable caught hold of him. Everything having been made ready, the signal was given, the fatal drop fell, and the unfortunate man was launched into eternity. Just before he was turned off, he said in a feeble tone, "I am justly sentenced, and may God forgive me"

The Murder of Maria Marten.
BY W. CORDER.

COME all you thoughtless young men, a warning take by me,
And think upon my unhappy fate to be hanged upon a tree;
My name is William Corder, to you I do declare,
I courted Maria Marten, most beautiful and fair.

I promised I would marry her upon a certain day,
Instead of that, I was resolved to take her life away,
I went into her father's house the 18th day of May,
Saying, my dear Maria, we will fix the wedding day.

If you will meet me at the Red-barn, as sure as I have life,
I will take you to Ipswich town, and there make you my wife;
I then went home and fetched my gun, my pickaxe and my spade,
I went into the Red-barn, and there I dug her grave.

With heart so light, she thought no harm, to meet him she did go
He murdered her all in the barn, and laid her body low ;
After the horrible deed was done, she lay weltering in her gore,
Her bleeding mangled body he buried beneath the Red-barn floor.

Now all things being silent, her spirit could not rest,
She appeared unto her mother, who suckled her at her breast,
For many a long month or more, her mind being sore oppress'd,
Neither night or day she could not take any rest.

Her mother's mind being so disturbed, she dreamt three nights o'er,
Her daughter she lay murdered beneath the Red-barn floor;
She sent the father to the barn, when he the ground did thrust,
And there he found his daughter mingling with the dust.

My trial is hard, I could not stand, most woeful was the sight,
When her jaw-bone was brought to prove, which pierced my heart quite ;
Her aged father standing by, likewise his loving wife,
And in her grief her hair she tore, she scarcely could keep life.

Adieu, adieu, my loving friends, my glass is almost run,
On Monday next will be my last, when I am to be hang'd ,
So you, young men, who do pass by, with pity look on me,
For murdering Maria Marten, I was hang'd upon the tree.

"Oh, she lives snug in the Holy Land,
  Right, tight, and merry in the Holy Land,
  Search the globe round, none can be found
  So *accommodating!* as Old Mother Cummins—of the Holy Land."

Catnach, like many others connected with the getting up of news broadsides and fly-sheets, did not always keep clear of the law. The golden rule is a very fine one, but, unfortunately, it is not always read aright; in some cases injured innocence flies at extremes. Jemmy Catnach for a long time had been living upon unfriendly terms with a party connected with the management of one of Mother Cummins's lodging-house establishments in the immediate neighbourhood, so out of spite printed a pamphlet, purporting to be the "Life and Adventures of Old Mother Cummins." Here Catnach had reckoned without his host, by reason of his not taking into consideration the extensive aristocratic and legal connection Mother Cummins had for her friends and patrons. The moment she was made acquainted with the *"dirty parjury"* that Jemmy Catnach had printed and caused to be publicly circulated, she immediately gave instructions to *her* Attorney-General to prosecute the *varmint*, when a warrant was applied for and obtained to search the premises of the Seven Dials printer. But Catnach got the news of the intended visit of the Bow Street Runners, and naturally became alarmed from having a vivid recollection of the punishment and costs in the case of the Drury-lane sausage makers, so the forme containing the libellous matter was at once broken up—" pied," that is, the type was jumbled together and left to be properly distributed on a future occasion. What stock of the pamphlets remained were hastily packed up and carried off to the "other side of the water" by John Morgan, one of Catnach's poets ! while another forme, consisting of a Christmas-sheet, entitled "The Sun of Righteousness," was hurriedly got to press, and all hands were working away full of assumed innocence when the officers from Bow Street arrived at Monmouth-court, when, after a diligent search, they had very reluctantly to come to the conclusion that they were "a day behind the fair," and that the printer had been a little too sharp for them this time. But Mother Cummins did not mean to be so checkmated by Catnach and Co., and vowed to pursue him and his dirty blackguards to the end of the world and back again, and instructed her lawyers to serve him with several notices of action for libel, defamation of character, and, more particular, as she expressed it, for *"parjury."* Then Catnach became somewhat alarmed by her known vindictive disposition and long purse, that he consulted his own solicitor in the matter, who took "counsel's opinion" when an instant compromise at all costs, together with an ample apology, was recommended as the only safe way out of the dilemma; a course which was ultimately agreed to by both sides. An apology was drawn up and approved of, with the understanding that Catnach was, after paying all costs incurred to print the apology and publish the same on three several places in front of his business premises in Monmouth Court for fourteen clear days. All this—and more—Jemmy promised steadfastly to observe. Yet in effect, he evaded the conditions by printing the apology in small pica type and sticking the three copies so high up on the premises, that it would have required Sam Weller's "pair of double million magnifying gas microscopes of hextra power" to have been able to read the same.

Immediately after Mother Cummins's death and funeral, March, 1828, the following announcement appeared :—

*Published this Day, **Price** Sixpence, embellished . **with** a humorous Coloured Plate.*

THE LIFE AND ADVENTURES OF
MOTHER CUMMINS,

The celebrated Lady Abbess of St. Giles's; with a curious Description, Regulations, &c., of her singular Establishment. An account of her Funeral, &c. Interspersed with numerous Anecdotes of Living Characters, Visitors of Mother Cummins's Nunnery,—Capt. Shiels and the Forty-four Nuns—Poll Hankey and Sir Charles Stanton,—Jane Sealey and an Illustrous Person, &c.—With an Account of some of the principal Nuns of the Establishment; particularly Mrs. Throgmorton and Lord Al. .n..y—Bell Chambers and the D... of Y...,—Miss Wilkinson and Captain Featherstone—Marianne Hempstead, the Scotch Beauty—Miss Weltern Davis and the Rev. Mr. H...l..y Be..rs..d —Mary Thomas, the Female Chimney-Sweep, and Captain T...t...s, &c.

THE HISTORY OF

THE TRIAL, SENTENCE, FULL CONFESSION, AND EXECUTION OF
BISHOP & WILLIAMS,
THE BURKERS.

BURKING AND BURKERS.

The month of November, 1831, will be recorded in the annals of crimes and cruelties as particularly pre-eminent, for it will prove to posterity that other wretches could be found base enough to follow the horrid example of Burke and his accomplice Hare, to entice the unprotected and friendless to the den of death for sordid gain.

The horrible crime of "Burking," or murdering the unwary with the intention of selling their bodies at a high price to the anatomical schools, for the purpose of dissection, has unfortunately obtained a notoriety which will not be soon or easily forgotten. It took its horrifying appellation from the circumstances which were disclosed on the trial of the inhuman wretch Burke, who was executed at Edinburgh in 1829, for having wilfully and deliberately murdered several persons for the sole purpose of profiting by the sale of their dead bodies.

APPREHENSION OF THE BURKERS.

On Tuesday, November 8th, four persons, viz., John Bishop, Thomas Williams, James May, and Michael Shield, were examined at Bow Street Police Office on the charge of being concerned in the wilful murder of an unknown Italian boy. From the evidence adduced, it appeared that May, alias Jack Stirabout, a known resurrection-man, and Bishop, a body-snatcher, offered at King's College a subject for sale, Shield and Williams having charge of the body in a hamper, for which they demanded twelve guineas. Mr Partridge, demonstrator of anatomy, who, although not in absolute want of a subject, offered nine guineas, but being struck with its freshness sent a messenger to the police station, and the fellows were then taken into custody, examined before the magistrates, when Shield was discharged and the others ultimately committed for trial.

THE TRIAL.

Friday, December 2nd, having been fixed for the trial of the prisoners charged with the murder of the Italian boy, the Court was crowded to excess so early as eight o'clock in the morning.

At nine o'clock the Deputy Recorder, Mr Serjeant

Arabin, came into the court, when the prisoners severally pleaded "Not Guilty."

The Jury were then sworn, and at ten o'clock Chief Justice Tindal, Mr Baron Vaughan, and Mr Justice Littledale entered the Court, with the Lord Mayor and Sheriffs.

The Bench was crowded with persons of rank, amongst whom was the Duke of Sussex.

Mr Bodkin having opened the case, Mr Adolphus proceeded to state to the Jury the leading facts, as they were afterwards stated in the evidence produced. The case for the prosecution having closed, the prisoners were called upon for their defence.

The prisoner Bishop in his defence stated that he was thirty-three years of age, and had followed the occupation of carrier till the last five years, during which he had occasionally obtained a livelihood by supplying surgeons with subjects. He most solemnly declared that he had never disposed of any body that had not died a natural death.

Williams' defence briefly stated that he had never been engaged in the calling of a resurrectionist, but had only by accident accompanied Bishop on the sale of the Italian boy's body.

May, in his defence, admitted that for the last six years he had followed the occupation of supplying the medical schools with anatomical subjects, but disclaimed ever having had anything to do with the sale of bodies which had not died a natural death. That he had accidentally met with Bishop at the Fortune of War public house on the Friday on which the body was taken for sale to Guy's Hospital.

At eight o'clock the jury retired to consider their verdict, and on their return they found the prisoners were Guilty of Murder.

The Recorder then passed the awful sentence upon them, "That" each of them be hanged on Monday morning, and their bodies be delivered over for dissection and anatomization."

The prisoners heard the sentence as they had the verdict, without any visible alteration. May raised his voice, and in a firm tone said, "I am a murdered man, gentlemen."

THE FULL CONFESSION OF BISHOP AND WILLIAMS.

On Saturday morning Williams addressed a note to Mr Wontner, stating that he and Bishop wanted particularly to see him and Dr. Cotton, the Ordinary. In the course of the interview which immediately followed, both prisoners made a full confession of their guilt, both exculpating May altogether from being party to any of the murders. Having received the confessions, Mr Wontner immediately waited upon Mr Justice Littledale and Baron Vaughan, and upon communicating to them the statements, they said they would at once see the Home Secretary on the subject.

On Sunday morning the Sheriffs visited all three of the prisoners in succession, and with the Under-Sheriffs were engaged between three and four hours in taking down the statements of the convicts. The result of all these investigations was that the same afternoon a respite during his Majesty's pleasure arrived at Newgate for May, and his sentence will be commuted to transportation for life.

THE EXECUTION.

During the whole of Sunday crowds of persons congregated in the Old Bailey, and the spot on which the scaffold was to be erected was covered with individuals conversing on the horrid crimes of the convicts, and in the course of the day strong posts were erected in the Old Bailey and at the ends of Newgate street, Giltspur street, and Skinner street, for the purpose of forming barriers to break the pressure of the crowd.

At half-past twelve o'clock the gallows was brought out from the yard, and drawn to its usual station opposite the Debtor's door. The crowd, as early as one o'clock amounting to several thousand persons, continued rapidly increasing.

By some oversight three chains had been suspended from the fatal beam, and this led the crowd to suppose that May had not been respited. Mr. Wontner, on hearing of the mistake, directed that one of the chains should be removed. The moment this was done an exclamation of "May is respited," ran through the crowd, and, contrary to the expected tokens of indignation, distinct cheers were heard amongst the crowd on witnessing this token that mercy had been shown to May.

At half-past seven the Sheriffs arrived in their carriage, and in a short time the press-yard was thronged with gentlemen. The unhappy convicts were now led from their cells. Bishop came out first, and after he was pinioned he was conducted to a seat, and the Rev. Mr. Williams sat alongside of him, and they conversed together in a low tone of voice.

Williams was next introduced, and the wonderful alteration two days had effected in his appearance astonished everyone who was present at the trial. All the bold confidence he exhibited then had completely forsaken him, and he looked the most miserable wretch it is possible to conceive. He entered the room with a very faltering step, and when the ceremony of pinioning him commenced, he was so weak as to be scarcely able to stand.

Everything being ready, the melancholy procession moved forward. Bishop was then conducted to the scaffold, and the moment he made his appearance the most dreadful yells and hootings were heard among the crowd. The executioner proceeded at once to the performance of his duty, and having put the rope round his neck and affixed it to a chain, placed him under the fatal beam. Williams was then taken out, and the groans and hisses were renewed. The dreadful preparations were soon completed, and in less than five minutes after the wretched men appeared on the scaffold the usual signal was given, the drop fell, and they were launched into eternity. Bishop appeared to die very soon, but Williams struggled hard. Thus died

THE DREADFUL BURKERS OF 1881.

It may be remarked, *en passant*, that Mr. Corder, with Paragalli and Colla, the two Italian witnesses, who gave evidence as to the identity of the body, said to be that of the Italian boy, at the trial of Bishop, Williams, and May, appeared at Bow Street, in consequence of doubts being entertained by a portion of the public as to the body being that of Carlo Ferrari, to re-assert their former evidence. Mr. Corder afterwards published a statement in the "Times" newspaper, which gave scarcely the possibility of doubt that the body offered at King's College *must have been* that of Ferrari notwithstanding the murderer's assertion to the contrary. On December the 10th, a *Post-obit* prosecution of Williams, the Burkite murderer, took place in the Court of Excise, where he was charged, on information, with having carried on an illicit factory for making glass at No. 2, Nova Scotia Gardens, Bethnal Green. An officer proved the seizure of goods used in the manufacture of glass, at the house of the person charged, and that Bishop was at the time in company. The Court condemned the goods seized.

A drama on the subject of the "Burkers" was produced at an unlicensed theatre, designated THE SHAKESPEARE, in the Kingsland Road, and not far from Shoreditch Church, and for a time was specially attractive. In the young actor, who played Carlo Ferrari, the Italian boy, might now be recognised an eminent tragedian.*

---

* E. L. Blanchard, in an article entitled, "Vanished Theatres," in the *Era Almanack*, 1877.

Street-ballads on political subjects, though not regarded as of great interest by the whole body of the people, are still eventful among certain classes, and for such the street author and ballad singer cater. The measure of Reform by Earl Grey's administration, was proposed in the House of Commons by Lord John Russell, 1st March, 1831. On the first division, *second* reading 22nd March, there stood for it, 302; against it, 301. Ultimately, the Bill for that session was abandoned, and Parliament dissolved. The Reform Bill of 1832 was read for the *third* time on the 23rd of March, when the numbers stood thus:—for the Bill, 355; against it, 239—majority for it, 116. In the Lords, the Bill was carried through the Committee on the 30th of May, and read a *third* time on the 4th of June. For the Bill, 106; against, 22—majority, 84.

During the whole of the time the Reform Bills of 1831-2 were before the Houses of Parliament, the "Catnach Press," in common with other printing offices that produced street-literature, was very busy in publishing, almost daily, songs and papers in ridicule of borough-mongering and of the various rotten boroughs then in existence, but which were entirely swept away by the passing of this Bill, fifty-six boroughs in England being disfranchised, while thirty were reduced to one member only; twenty-two new boroughs were created to send two members, and twenty to send one member; other important changes were also made. Songs upon the subject were sung at every corner of the streets, to the great delight of the multitude.

The Reform Bill.

As William and *Bill* are the same,
  Our King, if he "weathers the storm,"
Shall be called in the annals of fame,
  The *Glorious* BILL *of Reform!*

ATTACK ON KING WILLIAM IV. AT ASCOT HEATH,
ON TUESDAY, THE 19TH OF JUNE, 1832.

The Ascot Races for 1832 will be rendered memorable in the history of this country by reason of a stone thrown at his Majesty while on the grand stand at Ascot Races, which hit him on the forehead. The man by whom it was thrown was immediately secured, and proved to be Dennis Collins, a seaman with only one leg, formerly a pensioner of Greenwich Hospital, from whence he had been dismissed for ill-conduct. On his examination he confessed he committed the outrage in revenge because no notice had been taken of petitions which he had sent to the Lords of the Admiralty and the King. He was committed to Reading gaol to take his trial, which took place at Abingdon, on August 22nd. The jury returned a verdict of guilty on the fifth count, that of intending some bodily harm to his Majesty, but not guilty of the intent to kill.

Mr. Baron Gurney passed sentence on the prisoner, that he *be drawn on a hurdle to the place of execution*, and being hung by his *neck* until dead, his *head* be afterwards *severed from his body*, and his body *divided into four pieces*, and disposed of as his Majesty should think fit. His sentence was afterwards respited.

Nothing better than the above circumstance could have suited the producers and workers of street-literature. King William and Queen Adelaide were very popular at the time. "Yes, sir, we all did well out of that job of the wooden-legged sailor and old King Billy. It lasted out for months. We had something fresh nearly every day. We killed old Billy five or six times; then we made out that the sailor-chap was a love-child of the Sailor King and Madame Vestris; then that he was an old sweetheart of Queen Adelaide's, and that he was jealous and annoyed at her a jilting of him and a-marrying of old King Billy, and so on. But it was an awful sell, and a robbery to us all, because they didn't hang and cut the chap up into four quarters —that would have been a regular Godsend to us chaps, sir. But I think old Jemmy Catnach, as it was, must have cleared pretty nigh or quite fifty pounds for himself out of the job. A-talking about Madame Vestris, sir, reminds me that once we had a song about her, and the chorus was:—

"'A hundred pounds reward
For the man that cut the legs above the knees
Belonging to Madame Vestris.'"

The year 1837 produced two sensational murders and executions. The first case—that of Pegsworth—made a great stir, particularly in the east part of London. It was on the evening of the 9th of January, 1837, that a most atrocious and cold-blooded murder was committed in Ratcliff Highway. The individual who suffered was Mr John Holliday Ready, who for some time carried on the trade of a tailor, draper, and milliner. John Pegsworth, was a messenger in the tea department of St. Katherine's Docks, he had formerly kept a small tobacconist's shop in the same street, and had contracted a debt of £1 with Mr. Ready, who being unable to obtain payment, took out a summons against him in the Court of Requests, Osborne-street, Whitechapel. The court gave judgement against Pegsworth for the full amount and costs, which he was ordered to pay by instalments. On the evening of the same day Pegsworth proceeded to a cutler's shop in Shadwell, where he bought a large pig-knife, armed with which he immediately repaired to the house of Mr. Ready for the purpose of executing his diabolical intention. He entered the shop, and having spoken to Mrs. Ready, passed on to the parlour and got into conversation with Mr. Ready. Pegsworth, although pressingly asked to do so, declined taking a seat, and after he had been talking about ten minutes in a calm and collected manner on the subject of the debt and the misfortunes he had met with in business, he pointedly asked Mr. Ready if he intended to enforce the payment of the debt? Ready said he should be compelled to issue an execution against his goods if the money was not paid. The words had scarcely left the lips of the unfortunate man than Pegsworth uttered some exclamation which is supposed to have been "Take that!" and plunged the knife with great force into his breast up to the hilt. Ready called out to his wife, "O, I am stabbed!" fell back in his chair, and almost immediately expired. Mrs. Ready, who saw Pegsworth move his arm, but was not aware her husband was stabbed until she saw him fall back, screamed aloud for assistance, and several of her neighbours rushed into the shop for the purpose of securing the murderer, who did not make the least attempt to escape, but having completed his purpose, withdrew the knife from the body of his victim, laid it on the table, and calmly awaited the arrival of the police.

Pegsworth was tried at the Central Criminal Court of London on the 12th of February, and found guilty of wilful murder, and was executed in front of the debtor's door in the Old Bailey on the 9th of March following.

During the whole of the time that was occupied in the trial and execution of Pegsworth, a circumstance took place which excited an extraordinary sensation throughout the metropolis and its neighbourhood—namely, the discovery near the Pine Apple Gate, Edgware Road, of the trunk of a human being, tied up in a sack, dismembered of the arms, legs, and head.

The utmost vigilance was exercised to trace out the murderer, but for several days no light was thrown upon the transaction. At length, on the 6th of January, as a barge was passing down the Regent's Canal, near Stepney, one of the eastern environs of London, the bargeman, to his unspeakable horror, fished up what proved to be a human head. Proper notice of this circumstance was forwarded to the police. It was now very generally supposed the head would prove to belong to the body found in the Edgware road, although at a distance of nearly five miles, and this conjecture proved to be correct.

On the second of February the remaining portions of the human being was discovered in a sack in an osier bed, near Cold Harbour Lane, Camberwell. These mutilated remains were carefully matched together, and at length recognised as those of a Mrs. Brown, and suspicion fell, and justly so, upon James Greenacre and his paramour Sarah Gale.

In respect to the last two murders we have cited, Mr. Henry Mayhew received from an old "running patterer" the following statement—"Pegsworth was an out-and-out lot. I did tremendous with him, because it happened in London, down Ratcliff Highway—that's a splendid quarter for working—there's plenty of feeling—but, bless you, some places you go to you can't move nohow, they've hearts like paving stones. They wouldn't have 'the papers' if you'd give them to 'em—especially when they knows you. Greenacre didn't sell so well as might have been expected, for such a diabolical out-and-out crime as he committed; but you see he came close after Pegsworth, and that took the beauty off him. Two murderers together is no good to nobody."

In the Greenacre tragedy Catnach did a great amount of business, and as it was about the last "popular murder" in which he had any trade concern, we give a statement in respect to the sale of "Execution Papers," of the chief modern *'popular'* murders, thus :—

Of Rush murder	2,500,000 copies.
Of the Mannings	2,500,000 ,,
Of Courvoisier	1,666,000 ,,
Of Greenacre	1,650,000 ,,
Of Corder (Maria Marten)	1,166,000 ,,
Of the Five Pirates (Flowery Land)	290,000 ,,
Of Müller	280,000 ,,

So that the printers and publishers of "Gallows" Literature in general, and "The Catnach Press" in particular must have reaped a golden harvest for many a long day, even when sold to the street patterers at the low rate of 3d. per *long* dozen.

LIFE, TRIAL, CONFESSION, & EXECUTION
OF
JAMES GREENACRE,
FOR THE
EDGEWARE ROAD MURDER.

On the 22nd of April, James Greenacre was found guilty of the wilful murder of Hannah Brown, and Sarah Gale with being accessary after the fact. A long and connected chain of evidence was produced, which showed, that the sack in which the body was found was the property of Mr. Ward; that it was usually deposited in a part of the premises which led to the workshop, and could without observation have been carried away by him; that the said sack contained several fragments of shavings of mahogany, such as were made in the course of business by Ward; and that it contained some pieces of linen cloth, which had been patched with nankeen; that this linen cloth matched exactly with a frock which was found on Greenacre's premises, and which belonged to the female prisoner. Feltham, a police-officer, deposed, that on the 24th of March he apprehended the prisoners at the lodgings of Greenacre; that on searching the trousers pocket of that person, he took therefrom a pawnbroker's duplicate for two silk gowns, and from the fingers of the female prisoner two rings, and also a similar duplicate for two veils, and an old-fashioned silver watch, which she was endeavouring to conceal; and it was further proved that these articles were pledged by the prisoners, and that they had been the property of the deceased woman.—Two surgeons were examined, whose evidence was most important, and whose depositions were of the greatest consequence in throwing a clear light on the manner in which the female, Hannah Brown, met with her death. Mr. Birtwhistle deposed, that he had carefully examined the head; that the right eye had been knocked out by a blow inflicted while the person was living; there was also a cut on the cheek, and the jaw was fractured, these two last wounds were, in his opinion, produced after death; there was also a bruise on the head, which had occurred after death; the head had been separated by cutting, and the bone sawed across although, and then broken off; there were the marks of a saw, which fitted with a saw which was found in Greenacre's box. Mr. Girdwood, a surgeon, very minutely and skilfully described the appearances presented on the head, and showed incontestibly, that the head had been severed from the body while the person was yet alive; that this was proved by the retraction, or drawing back, of the muscles at the parts where they were separated by the knife, and further, by the blood-vessels being empty, the body was drained of blood. This part of the

evidence produced a thrill of horror throughout the court, but Greenacre remained quite unmoved.

After a most impressive and impartial summing up by the learned Judge, the jury retired, and, after the absence of a quarter of an hour, returned into court, and pronounced a verdict of "Guilty" against both the prisoners.

The prisoners heard the verdict without evincing the least emotion, or the slightest change of countenance. After an awful silence of a few minutes, the Lord Chief Justice said they might retire, as they would be remanded until the end of the session.

They were then conducted from the bar, and on going down the steps, the unfortunate female prisoner kissed Greenacre with every mark of tenderness and affection.

The crowd outside the court on this day was even greater than on either of the preceding; and when the result of the trial was made known in the street, a sudden and general shout succeeded, and continued huzzas were heard for several minutes.

THE EXECUTION.

At half past seven the sheriff arrived in his carriage, and in a short time the press-yard was thronged with gentlemen who had been admitted by tickets. The unhappy convict was now led from his cell. When he arrived in the press-yard, his whole appearance portrayed the utmost misery and spirit-broken dejection, his countenance haggard, and his whole frame agitated; all that self-possession and fortitude which he displayed in the early part of his imprisonment, had utterly forsaken him, and had left him a victim of hopelessness and despair. He requested the executioner to give him as little pain as possible in the process of pinioning his arms and wrists; he shivered not a word in allusion to his crime; neither did he make any dying request, except that his spectacles might be given to Sarah Gale; he exhibited no sign of hope; he shewed no symptom of communication with the offended God! When the venerable ordinary preceded him in the solemn procession through the vaulted passage to the fatal drop, he was so prostrate and unmanned, that he could not support himself without the aid of the assistant executioner. At the moment he ascended the scaffold, from which he was to be launched into eternity, the most terrible yell, groans, and cheers were vociferated by the immense multitude surrounding the place of execution. Greenacre bowed to the sheriff, and begged he might not be allowed to remain long in the suspense; and almost immediately the fatal bolt was withdrawn, and, without a struggle, he became a lifeless corse.—Thus ended the days of Greenacre, a man endowed with more than ordinary talents, repeatedly commended, and deservedly placed in society; but a want of probity, an absolute dearth of principle, led him on from one crime to another, until at length he perpetrated the sanguinary deed which brought his career to an awful and disgraceful period, and which he enrolled his name among the most notorious of those who have expiated their crime on the gallows.

On hearing the death-bell toll, Gale became dreadfully agitated, and when she heard the brutal shouts of the crowd of spectators, she fainted, and remained in a state of alternate mental agony and insensibility throughout the whole day.

After having been suspended the usual time, his body was cut down, and buried in a hole dug in one of the passages of the prison, near the spot where, Thistlewood and his associates were interred.

Catnach received a very indifferent education, and that little at the establishment of Mr. Goldie, in Alnwick, where his attendance was very irregular, and this drawback assisted very much in blunting his relish for the higher walks of literature. The father had not carried out the heavenly injunction so much practised in Scotland, by giving to his son the best of blessings —"a good education."

Jemmy had a tenacious love of money, and this propensity he retained throughout life. As a man of business he was rough and brusque in his manners, but this mattered little, as his trade lay amongst a class who were low and insensitive in their habits and modes of living.

The productions issued at the "Catnach Press" were not destined to rank high in the annals of literature; and they bear a sorry appearance when placed alongside of several works of a similar kind, which were printed at the same period in many parts of the kingdom. In this respect Jemmy Catnach was very unlike his father, for, whilst the former had a niggardly turn in all his dealings, the latter was naturally inclined to the reverse.

One class of literature which Jemmy Catnach made—by reason of greater mechanical skill and a larger capital than his rivals—almost his own, was children's farthing, halfpenny, and penny books. Among the great many that he published we select from our own private collection, those that follow as a fair sample.

Many other nursery books of a similar kind might be mentioned as some of the chief attractions that emanated from the "Catnach Press," and which, to the juvenile population, were more eagerly welcomed than the great sensational three-volume novels are by many in our day.

"THE CATNACH PRESS."

A

COLLECTION

OF

JUVENILE BOOKS.

PRINTED AND PUBLISHED BY

JAMES CATNACH,

LATE OF

MONMOUTH COURT,

SEVEN DIALS,

LONDON.

Nurse Love-Child's
LEGACY

LONDON:
Printed by J. Catnach, 2, Monmouth
Court, 7 Dials.

2

The Lion and the unicorn,
Were fighting for the crown,
The lion beat the unicorn,
All round about the town,
Some gave them white bread
And some gave them brown,
Some gave them plum cake
And sent them out of town.

3

NURSE LOVECHILD'S LEGACY.

What is the news of the day,
Good neighbour I pray,
They say the bailoon,
Is gone up to the moon.

NURSE LOVECHILD'S LEGACY.

The little mouse
Doth skip and play,
He runs by night,
And sleeps by day.

5

NURSE LOVECHILD'S LEGACY.

This is the Cat
That killed the Cock,
For waking her
At five o'clock.

6

NURSE LOVECHILD'S LEGACY.

And this is the Dog
That bit the thief,
For stealing all
His master's beef.

7

NURSE LOVECHILD'S LEGACY.

Who comes here
A Grenadier,
What do you want
A pot of beer,
Where's **your money**
I've forgot.
Get you gone
You drunken sot.

8

NURSE LOVECHILD'S LEGACY.

Be not a glutton when you eat,
But spare some for the needy,
Or people will, when filled with meat,
Say, like a wolf, you are greedy.

9

NURSE LOVECHILD'S LEGACY.

There **was a** little **man,**
And he had a little gun,
And his bullets were made of lead,
He shot John Sprig
Thro' the middle of his wig,
And knock'd it off his head.

10

NURSE LOVECHILD'S LEGACY.

Now what do you think
Of little Jack Jingle,
Before he was married,
He used to live single.
But after he **married**,
To alter his life,
He left off living single
And lived with his wife

11

NURSE LOVECHILD'S LEGACY.

Tom Trueby was a good and sensible boy, who neither played the truant nor kept company with naughty children. He did not like tossing up nor chuck up farthing, because he thought it might lead him to love gaming, when he was grown up; but he liked very well to play at ball or top, and most particularly at marbles, at which he was very clever, never cheated, and played so well that he used to teach the neighbouring children.

12

NURSE LOVECHILD'S LEGACY.

And here you see him instructing Master Manly, a Baronet's son in the place, as he did in matters of more consequence, and behaved so well towards him, that he was his friend all his lifetime.

13

NURSE LOVECHILD'S LEGACY.

Fire-Works and Crackers.

Fire-Works are things that look very pretty when they are properly managed by those who understand them, but children ought to take care how they meddle with gunpowder lest they should hurt themselves or other people.

14

NURSE LOVECHILD'S LEGACY.

Tom Hazard for example was always fond of playing with serpents crackers &c. At one time he was near doing damage by his fireworks falling into a cellar, and at another time as you see in the cut he so much frightened one of his schoolfellows that he fell down, and put his ancle out, for which Tom was severely corrected and you must own he richly deserved it.

NURSE LOVECHILD'S LEGACY.

See the Mother,
Good and mild,
How she plays
With her dear Child.

NURSE LOVECHILD'S LEGACY.

See the Maid
 By kindness led,
To feed the Fowls
 With crumbs of bread.

FINIS.

J. Catnach, Printer.

THE GOLDEN PIPPIN.

LONDON:
Printed by J. Catnach,
2, Monmouth-
Court, 7 Dials.

2

The
Lord's Prayer.

Our Father, who art in Heaven, hallowed be thy Name, thy Kingdom come, thy Will be done on Earth, as it is in Heaven, Give us this Day our daily Bread, and forgive us our Trespasses as we forgive them that trespass against us, and lead us not into Temptation, but deliver us from Evil. For thine is the Kingdom, the power and the Glory, for ever and ever. Amen.

3

A
Was an Arch Boy.

B
A Beauty was.

4

C
A comely Wench but Coy.

D
A Dainty Lass.

5

E
Loved Eggs, and eat his fill.

F
Was full and fat.

118 THE HISTORY OF

6

G
Had Grace and wit at will.

H
Wore a Gold Lace Hat.

7

I
Stands for little Jackys name.

K
For Kitty Fair.

S

L
Loved Learning & got fame.

M
Was his Mother dear.

9

N
Was naughty & oft crying.

O
An Only Child.

10

P
Was pretty Peggy sighing.

Q
Was a Quaker mild,

R
Was Rude, & in disgrace.

S
Stands for Sammy Still.

124   THE HISTORY OF

12

T
For ever talked a-pace.

V
Was fond of Veal.

13

W
He watched the house & hall.

X
Does like a Cross appear.

126   THE HISTORY OF

14

Y
A Youth well shaped & tall.

Z
Whips up the Rear.

15

Let all good children come to me,
And I'll learn them their
  A B C

A	*A*	J	*J*	S	*S*
B	*B*	K	*K*	T	*T*
C	*C*	L	*L*	U	*U*
D	*D*	M	*M*	V	*V*
E	*E*	N	*N*	W	*W*
F	*F*	O	*O*	X	*X*
G	*G*	P	*P*	Y	*Y*
H	*H*	Q	*Q*	Z	*Z*
I	*I*	R	*R*		

& which stands for and

And when your Great Letters you
　　know,
Then I'll teach you the Small also.

J. Catnach, Printer.

JERRY DIDDLE,
AND HIS
FIDDLE.

*If you are bad | And praise will all
I pray reform, | Your acts adorn.*

London:
Printed by J. Catnach, 2, Monmouth
Court, 7 Dials.

2

JERRY DIDDLE.
Bought a fiddle,
To play to little boys,
He wax'd his string,
And began to sing,
Youth is the time for joys.

He went to a pig, and play'd a jig.

3

The pigs did grunt for joy,
 Till the farmer came out,
 And made a great rout, (boy,"
Saying "Off, or I'll cane you, my

He met an old woman to market
 a prancing,   (a dancing.
He took out his fiddle, and set her

4

She broke all her eggs,
  And dirtied her butter;
At which her old husband
  Began for to splutter.

Oh! then, said Jerry,
I'll soon make you merry.

5

And the way with his fiddle he
 led,
The old man heard the tune,
As he sat in his room,

And danc'd on top of his
 head.

6

He next met a barber,
   With powder and wig,

He play'd him a tune,
   And he shaved an old pig.

7

Then up in his arms
He carried the boar,

And went to the ale-house,
To dance on the floor.

8

He met an old man,
  With beer in a can,
And a bundle of clothes on his shoulder,

He bade Jerry play,
  And threw all away,
To astonish each gaping beholder.

9

He went to a tailor,
  Who was ill in bed;

When he got up to dance,
  With a goose on his head.

10

He went to a fishwomen,
Tippling of gin,

When she like a top,
Began for to spin.

11

The publican star'd,
    As he fill'd out the glasses,

But when Jerry play'd,
    He danc'd with the lasses.

12

He next met an old man,
With beard white and long,

Who laugh'd at poor Jerry,
And scoff'd at his song.

13

His name was Instruction,
The friend of the wise,

Who teaches good youth,
To win honor's prize.

14

He broke Jerry's fiddle,
 And taught him to read,

And told him that honor
 Would daily succeed.

15

Jerry now is a lad
  At school always true,

The joy of his friends,
  And a pattern for you.

Be instructed by him,
To avoid folly's snare,

And your bosom thro' life,
Will escape every care.

FINIS.

JUMPING JOAN.

Here am I, little
Jumping Joan,
When nobody's with me,
I'm always alone.

London.
Printed by J. Catnach, 2, Monmouth
Court, 7 Dials.

2

Jumping Joan.

Joan had a dog, and
Joan had a cat,
Look at them both, see
How pretty they're sat.

3

Jumping Joan.

Joan she lov'd skipping,
And was not at a loss,
At jumping or hopping,
Or going a cross.

4

Jumping Joan.

Joan had a parrot
Could chatter and bawl,
But Joan could talk faster,
And longer withal.

5

Jumping Joan.

Joan's dog, Prinny,
No learning did lack,
He'd carry Poll in his mouth
And Puss on his back.

6

Jumping Joan.

As Joan lov'd jumping,
She learned her cat,
Look at them both,
And see what they're at.

7

Jumping Joan.

Here's Pussy a washing
Joan's linen you know,
She could wash for herself
A long while ago.

8

Jumping Joan.

Now Prinny, Joan's dog,
To market would go,
But what he'll bring back,
I'm sure I don't know.

9

Jumping Joan.

Here's Pussy drest out
Like a lady so gay,
She's going to court, if
She finds but the way.

10

Jumping Joan.

Here's Prinny and Pussy
To dancing have got,
While Joan plays a tune
On the lid of a pot.

11

Jumping Joan.

Here's Joan with a whip,
Taking very long strides,
And vows if she finds 'em,
She'll bang both their hides

12

Jumping Joan.

Here's Prinny with gun,
Sword and gorget so smart,
He's going to France,
To fight Bonaparte.

13

Jumping Joan.

And **Joan's** threat had fill'd
Poor Prin with alarms,
He said he'd not fight,
And so grounded his arms.

14

Jumping Joan.

Then Puss in a fright
Ran back to the house,
She pull'd off her clothes,
And has just caught a mouse

15

Jumping Joan.

Then Joan she came in,
Call'd the cat saucy puss,
And said Prin was a puppy,
To frighten her thus.

Jumping Joan.

They fell on their knees,
Her pardon to crave,
And promis'd in future,
They'd better behave.

J. Catnach, Printer.

This Milk Maid and
Book for a halfpenny.

TO THE
Juvenile Reader.

Little Boys and Girls will find
At Catnach's something to their mind.
From great variety may choose,
What will instruct them and amuse;
The prettiest plates that you can find,
To please at once the eye and mind,
In all his little books appear,
In natural beauty, shining clear,
Instruction unto youth when given,
Points the path from earth to heaven.

He sells by Wholesale and Retail,
To suit all moral tastes can't fail.

THE
Butterfly's Ball,
AND
Grasshopper's Feast.

Come take up your hats,
  And away let us haste,
To the Butterfly's Ball,
  Or the Grasshopper's Feast.

J. Catnach,
2, Monmouth Court, 7 Dials.

THE
BUTTERFLY'S BALL
AND
Grasshopper's Feast.

The trumpeter Gad-fly,
   Has summon'd the crew,
And the revels are now,
   Only waiting for you.

On the smooth shaved grass,
   By the side of a wood,
Beneath a broad oak,
   Which for ages had stood.

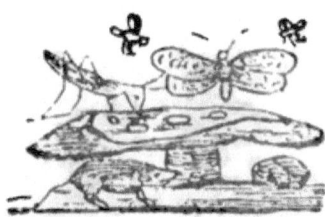 

See the children of earth,
   And the tenants of air,
To an evening's amusement,
   Together repair.

And there came the Beetle,
   So blind and so black,
And carried the Emmet,
   His friend on his back.

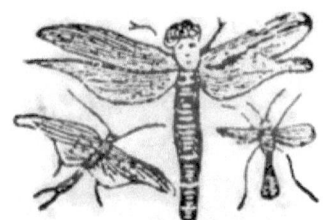 

And there came the Gnat,
   And the Dragon-fly too,
And all their relations—
   Green, orange and blue.

And there came the Moth
   With her plume of down,
And the Hornet with jacket
   Of yellow and brown.

Who with him the Wasp,
    His companion did bring,
But they promised that evening
    To lay by their sting.

The sly little Dormouse,
    Peep'd out of his hole,
And led to the feast,
    His blind cousin the Mole.

And the Snail with his horns,
    Peeping out of a shell.
Came fatigued with the distance,
    The length of an ell.

A Mushroom the table,
    And on it was spread,
A water-dock leaf,
    Which their table-cloth made.

The viands were various,
  To each of their taste,
And the Bee brought the honey,
  To sweeten the feast.

With steps most majestic,
  The Snail did advance,
And he promised the gazers
  A minuet to dance.

But they all laugh'd so loud,
  That he drew in his head,
And went in his own
  Little chamber to bed.

Then as the evening gave way
  To the shadows of night,
Their watchman the glow-worm
  Came out with his light.

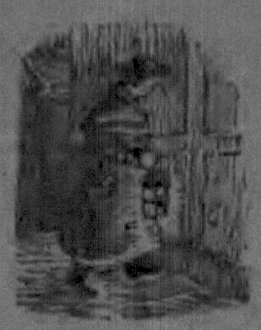

So home let us hasten,
While yet we can see,
For no watchman is waiting,
For you or for me.

J. Crouch, Printer.

A halfpenny Pay
and take honest Tray.

Let all good children come to me,
And I'll learn them their

A B C

A	*A*	J	*J*	S	*S*
B	*B*	K	*K*	T	*T*
C	*C*	L	*L*	U	*U*
D	*D*	M	*M*	V	*V*
E	*E*	N	*N*	W	*W*
F	*F*	O	*O*	X	*X*
G	*G*	P	*P*	Y	*Y*
H	*H*	Q	*Q*	Z	*Z*
I	*I*	R	*R*		

& which stands for and

A Was an Archer and shot at a frog,
But missing his mark shot into a bog.

D Was a Drunkard and lov'd a full pot,
His face and his belly shew'd him a great sot.

B Was a Butcher and had a great dog,
Who always went round the streets with a clog.

E Was an Esquire, both lofty and proud,
His servant was softy though he was full loud.

C Was a Captain so brave and so grand,
He headed in buff the stately train'd band.

F Was a Farmer and followed the plough,
And gathered good from the sweat of his brow.

G Was a Gamester, and oft would he play,
A poor single ace against a bold tray.

J Was a Joiner and built him a house,
A little time after there came in a mouse.

H Hunted the buck, and likewise the doe,
The hart and the fox, and also the roe.

K Was a King, who would drink and carouse,
Affrighted was he at a stand and a mouse.

I Was an Image set up at Rome,
Many that see it were better at home.

L Was a Lady that lov'd a fine tree,
Though none understood it so little as she.

M Was a Merchant to foreign lands gone, To bring home fine tea and rich silks anon.

P Was a Parson, and wore a black gown, For goodness and virtue of high renown.

N Was a Noble of birth and high power, To the poor most gentle, to the haughty most sour.

O Was a Quaker, both stiff and upright, In yea and nay they chiefly delight.

O With her Oysters, a delicate cry. Come buy my sweet Oyster, come buy, come buy.

R Was a Robber on the highway, For which he's been hung this many a day.

S Was a Sailor and liv'd in a ship,
He made the Spaniards and French for to skip.

V Was a Vintner that loved his pottle,
Went seldom to bed without his full bottle.

T Was Tom Tinker and mended a kettle,
While he was hammering was deaf as a beetle.

W Was a Watchman, to guard the warehouse,
That rogues did not strip it of every souse.

U Was an Undertaker at work for his bread.
The living must pay, though he works for the dead.

X Was expensive, and so became poor,
With his little dog begged from door to door.

Y Was a Youngster that lov'd not his school,
But trundled his hoop though out of all rule.

Z Was a Zany that look'd like a fool,
With his long tassell'd cap he was the boy's fool.

And when your great letters you know,
Then I'll teach you the small ones also.

Printed by J. Catnach.

THE
Tragical Death
OF AN
Apple Pie,

Who was Cut to Pieces
AND EATEN BY
Twenty-Five Gentlemen,
WITH WHOM
All Little People
OUGHT TO BE ACQUAINTED

PRINTED BY J. PAUL & Co.,
LONDON;
2 & 3, Monmouth Court,

AN apple pie when it looks nice,
Would make one long to have a slice,
And if its taste should prove so too,
I fear one slice would scarcely do,
So to prevent my asking twice,
Pray mamma, cut a good large slice.

THE LIFE AND DEATH OF AN APPLE PIE.

A
An Apple-pie.

B
Bit it.

C
Cut it.

D
Dealt it.

E
Did eat it.

F
Fought for it.

180   THE HISTORY OF

    G   H   J   K
Got it.   Had it.   Join'd for it.   Kept it.

    L   M   N   O
Long'd for it. Mourned for it. Nodded at it. Open'd it.

P   Q   R   S
Peeped into it.   Quartered it.   Ran for it.   Stole it.

T   V   W   XYZ and &
Took it.   View'd it.   Wanted it.   All wished for
                                                      a piece in hand.

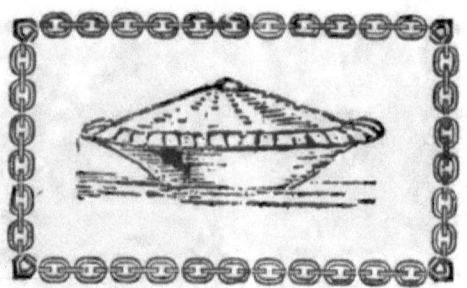

At last they every one agreed,
Upon the apple pie to feed;
But as there seem'd to be so many,
Those who were last might not have any,
Unless some method there was taken
That every one might have their bacon,
They all agreed to stand in order,
Around the apple pie's fine border,
Take turn as they in hornbook stand
From great A down to &,
In equal parts the pie divide,
As you may see on the other side.

A curious Discourse that passed between the Twenty-five Letters at dinner time.

A 1. Says, A, give me a good large slice
B 2. Says B, a little bit but nice.
C 3. Says C, cut me a piece of crust.
D 4. Take it, says D, 'tis dry as dust.
E 5. Says E, I'll eat it fast, who will?
F 6. Says F, I vow I'll have my fill.
G 7. Says G, give it me both good and great.
H 8. Says H, a little bit I hate.
I 9. Says I, I love the juice the best.
K 10. And K, the very same confess'd.
L 11. Says L, there's nothing more I love.
M 12. Says M, it makes your teeth to move.
N 13. N notic'd what the others said,
O 14. O, others plates with grief survey'd.
P 15. P prais'd the cook up to the life.
Q 16. Q quarrell'd because he'd a bad knife.
R 17. Says R, it runs short I'm afraid.
S 18. S, silent sat and nothing said.
T 19. T, thought that talking might lose time.
U 20. U understood it at meals a crime.
W 21. W wish'd there had been a quince in.
X 22. Says X, those cooks there's no convincing
Y 23 Says Y, I'll eat, let others wish.
Z 24. Z sat as mute as any fish.
& 25. While & he lick'd the dish.

Having concluded their discourse and dinner together, I have nothing more to add; but if my little readers are pleased with what they have found in this book they have nothing to do but to run to J. Paul & Co's., 2, & 3, Monmouth Court; 7 Dials, where they may have a great variety of books not less entertaining than this of the same size and price.

But that you may not think I leave you too abruptly, I here present you with the picture of dame Dumpling, who made the Apple pie you have

been reading about; she has several more in her basket, and she promised that if you are good children you shall never go to bed supperless while she has one left. But as good people always ask a blessing, as a token that you are good and deserve a pie, you must learn the two following Graces, that one be said before your meals, and the other after.

Grace before Meat.

GOOD Lord, bless us, and these thy creatures, to our use, which we are about to receive, of thy bounteous liberality, through Jesus Christ our Lord. Amen.

Grace after Meat.

WE thank thee, O Lord, for all the benefits of this time, and of our whole lives. Make us thankful for all thy mercies now, and for evermore. Amen.

THE
TEN COMMANDMENTS

PUT INTO SHORT RHYME.

1. Thou shalt have no other God but me.
2. Before no idol bow thy knee.
3. Take not the name of God it vain.
4. Nor dare the Sabbath-day profane.
5. Give both thy parents honour due.
6. Take heed that thou no murder do.
7. Abstain from words and deeds unclean.
8. Steal not, tho' thou art poor and mean.
9. Tell not a wilful lie, nor love it.
10. What is thy neighbour's, dare not covet.

J. Paul & Co., Printers,

OLD MOTHER HUBBARD AND HER WONDERFUL DOG.

Old Mother Hubbard went to the cupboard
   To get the poor dog a bone;
But when she came there the cupboard was bare,
   And so the poor dog had none.

LONDON:
Printed by J CATNACH, 2 & 3, Manmouth Court, 7 Dials.

She went to the baker's to buy him some bread,
When she came back the dog was dead.
Ah! my poor dog, she cried, oh, what shall I do?
You were always my pride—none equal to you.

She went to the undertaker's to buy him a coffin,
When she came back, the dog was laughing.
Now how this can be quite puzzles my brain,
I am much pleased to see you alive once again.

She went to the barber's to buy him a wig,
When she came back he was dancing a jig.
O, you dear merry grig, how nicely you're prancing;
Then she held up the wig, and he began dancing.

She went to the sempstress to buy him some linen,
When she came back the dog was spinning.
The reel, when 'twas done, was wove into a shirt,
Which served to protect him from weather and dirt.

To market she went, to buy him some tripe,
When she came back he was smoking his pipe.
Why, sure, cried the dame, you'd beat the great Jocko.
Who before ever saw a dog smoking tobacco?

She went to the alehouse to buy him some beer,
When she came back he sat on a chair.
Drink hearty, said Dame, there's nothing to pay,
'Twill banish your sorrow and moisten your clay.

She went to the fruiterer's to buy him some fruit,
When she came back he was playing the flute.
Oh, you musical dog, you surely can speak:
Come, sing me a song, then he set up a squeak.

She went to the tavern for white wine and red,
When she came back he stood on his head.
This is odd, said the dame, for fun you seem bred,
One would almost believe you'd wine in your head.

The dog he cut capers, and turned out his toes,
'Twill soon cure the vapours, he such attitude shows.
The dame made a curtsey, the dog made a bow,
The dame said, Your servant, the dog said Bow wow

THE
Royal Book.

OF
Nursery Rhymes.

A present for Little Masters and Misses.
A Good Book to Instruct and Amuse.

PUSSY-CAT, pussy-cat, where have you been?
I've been up to London to look at the queen.
Pussy-cat, pussy-cat, what did you there?
I frighten'd a little mouse under the chair.

London:
Published by RYLE and PAUL,
2 & 3, Monmouth Court, Seven Dials.

NURSERY RHYMES.

See-saw, sacradown,
Which is the way to London town?
One foot up, and the other down,
And that is the way to London town.

Hey diddle, the cat and the fiddle,
 The cow jumped over the moon.
The little dog laughed to see the
  sport,
And the dish ran away with the
  spoon.

Ding, dong, bell!
Pussy's in the well.
Who put her in?
Little Johnny Green.
Who pulled her out?
Little Johnny Snout,
What a naughty boy was that,
To drown poor pussy cat,
Who never did him any harm,
And kill'd the mice in his father's
  barn.

Jack and Jill went up the hill,
 To get a pail of water:
Jack fell down and broke his crown,
 And Jill came tumbling after.

Cock'a doodle do,
The dame has lost her shoe,
And master's lost his fiddle stick
And don't know what to do.

Simple Simon met a pieman,
  Going to the fair!
Says Simple Simon to the pieman,
  Let me taste your ware.

Says the pieman unto Simon
  First give me a penny;
Says Simple Simon to the pieman,
  I have not got any.

Once Simon made a great snow ball
  And brought it in to roast,
He laid it down before the fire,
  And soon the ball was lost.

He went to ride a spotted cow,
  That had a little calf,
She threw him down upon the ground
  And made all the people laugh.

Now Simple Simon went a fishing,
  For to catch a whale,
But all the water he had got
  Was in his mother's pail.

He went to catch a dickey bird
  And thought he could not fail
Because he had a bit of salt,
  To put upon his tail.

He went to see if cherries ripe,
  Did grow upon a thistle,
He pricked his finger very much,
  Which made poor Simon whistle.

He went to take a bird's nest,
  'Twas built upon a bough,
A branch gave way, down Simon fell
  Into a dirty slough.

Simon was sent to market,
　To buy a joint of meat,
He tied it to his horse's tail,
　To keep it clean and sweet.

He went to slide upon the ice,
　Before the ice would bear,
Then he plunged in above his knees,
　Which made poor Simon stare.

He went to shoot a wild duck,
　But the duck flew away,
Says Simon I can't hit him,
　Because he would not stay.

Then Simple Simon went a hunting,
　For to catch a hare,
He rode an ass about the street,
　But could not find one there.

He went for water in a seive,
　But soon it all run through,
And went all o'er his clothes,
　Which made poor Simon rue.

He washed himself with blacking ball,
　Because he had no soap,
And then said to his mother
　I'm a beauty now I hope.

He went to eat some honey,
　Out of the mustard pot,
It bit his tongue until he cried,
　That was all the good he got.

Simple Simon cutting his mother's bellows open to see where the wind lay.

JACK JINGLE.

Little Jack Jingle,
Played truant at school,
They made his bum tingle
For being a fool;
He promised no more
Like a fool he would look
But be a good boy and
  attend to his book.

See little Jack Jingle
  Learning his task,
He's a very good boy,
  If the neighbours should ask,
To school he does run,
  And no truant does play,
But when school is done,
  He can laugh and be gay.

Here sulky Sue,
  What shall we do.
Turn her face to the wall,
  Till she comes to;
If that should fail,
  A touch with the cane
Will do her good,
  When she feels the pain.

Now Suky never pouts,
  Never frowns, never flouts,
But reads her book with glee,
  Then dances merrily,
  No girl so good as she,
  In all the country;
Cheerfully doth all things do,
She lost the name of sulky Sue.

Jack Jingle went 'prentice,
  To make a horse-shoe,
He wasted the iron,
  Till it would not do,
His master came in,
  And began for to rail;
Says Jack, the shoe's spoil'd,
  But 'twill still make a nail.

Suke Shingle when young,
  Did what others have done,
She could dirty two clouts,
  While her mother wash'd one.
But now grown a stout wench,
  With her pail and her mop,
If she don't clean the board,
  She can make a great slop.

Little Jack Jingle,
  Went to court Suky Shingle,
Says he, shall we mingle
  Our toes in the bed;
Fye! Jacky Jingle,
  Says little Suke Shingle,
We must try to mingle,
  Our pence for some bread.

Suky you shall be my wife,
  And I'll tell you why;
I have got a little pig,
  And you have got a sty;
I have got a dun cow,
  And you can make good cheese,
Suky will you have me?
  Say yes, if you please.

DEATH & BURIAL OF COCK ROBIN.

Who kill'd Cock Robin?
  I said the sparrow,
  With my bow and arrow.
I kill'd Cock Robin.

Who caught his blood?
  I, said the fish,
  With my little dish—
I caught his blood.

This is the fish
That held the dish.

Who saw him die?
  I, said the fly
  With my little eye—
I saw him die.

This is the fly
That saw him die.

Who made his shroud?
  I, said the beetle,
  With my little needle—
I made his shroud.

This is the beetle,
With his little needle.

Who'll be the Parson?
I, said the rook,
With my little book—
I will be the Parson.

Here is Parson Rook,
Reading his book.

Who'll carry the coffin?
I, said the Kite,
If it's not in the night—
I'll carry the coffin

Behold the Kite,
How he takes his flight.

Who'll be the clerk?
I, said the Lark,
If its not in the dark—
I will be the clerk.

Behold how the Lark,
Says Amen like a clerk.

Who will carry the link?
I, said the linnet:
I'll fetch it in a minute—
I will carry the link.

The Linnet with a light,
Altho' it is not night.

LITTLE RED RIDING HOOD.

And now her riding hood is on,
   How pretty she does look;
Mamma made it to keep her warm
   Because she learn'd her book:
So be good girls all who hear this
   And boys be good also,
And your *Mammas* will give you all
   Great coats and hoods, I know.

The morning come—the hood put on,
   The pot and cake she took,
Biddy, good bye—good bye, *mamma*
   And then her hand she shook:
And so set off for *grandmamma's*
   Mamma stood at the door,
And watched her little *Biddy* till
   She could see her no more.

You see this pot of butter nice,
   And likewise this plum-cake,
Which little *Biddy's* dear *mamma*
   For *grandmamma* did make:
Who lived in a little house,
   A mile or two away,
And *Red Riding Hood* must take them,
   To *Grandmamma* next day

Now in the road to *grandma's* house,
   A lonesome wood there lay,
And *Goffip Wolf* popp'd from a bush,
   And stopp'd her in the way
He was a fierce and cruel beast,
   And would have eat her there,
But turning of his head about,
   He found he did not dare.

I'm going to my *grandmamma's*,
  She is not very well,
With cake and pot of butter;
  Says *Wolf* where does she dwell?
In yonder house, by yonder mill
  Good bye—I cannot stay—
And with her pretty finger, she
  Pointed out the way.

Now *grandmamma* being very ill,
  She on the bed did lie,
And called out, the bobbin pull,
  And up the latch will fly;
The bobbin pull'd, up flew the latch,
  The *Wolf* popp'd in his head
And soon he eat up *grandmamma*
  And then got into bed.

The *Wolf* got first to *grandma's* door,
  And knocked toc, toc, toc;
Who is that, said *grandmamma*,
  That at the door doth knock;
'Tis your *grandaughter*, said the *Wolf*,
  And mimic'd *Biddy's* voice,
Mamma has sent you a plumb cake,
  And pot of butter nice.

Toc, toc, toc, at *grandma's* door
  Knocked *Little Red Riding Hood*,
Who's there, says *Wolf*, and with a voice,
  Like *grandma's* as he could;
'Tis your *grandaughter*, little *Bid*
  With cake and pot of butter;
The bobbin pull, the latch will fly,
  The wicked *Wolf* did mutter.

CINDERELLA.

Here Cinderella you may see
　A beauty bright and fair,
Her real name was Helena,
　Few with her could compare
Besides she was so very good,
　So affable and mild,
She learned to pray and read
　　her book,
　Like a very good child.

Her mother-in-law you see,
　One of the worst of hags,
Who made her do all drudgery
　　work.
　And clothed her in rags;
And after she had done her
　　work,　　(tell her
　Her mother-in-law would
The cinders she might sit a-
　　mong,
　Then call'd her Cinderella.

These are her two sisters-in-law,
　Both deformed & ordinary,
Altho' they dress as fine as
　　queens,
　Which you may think ex-
　　traordinary;　　(read,
But neither of them scarce can
　Nor pray to God to bless 'em
They only know to patch and
　　paint,
　And gaudily to dress 'em.

This is the king's fine gallant
　　son,
　Young, handsome, straight
　　and tall
He invited all the ladies round
　For to dance at his ball;
Which when the ugly sisters
　　heard
　They dress'd themselves so fine,
And off they set, being resolv'd
　At this grand ball to shine.

Her god-mother came to **lend**
  her aid,
And her power is not small
To help her god-daughter to go
  To this fine prince's ball.
This coach was once a pump-
  kin, (that,
By the fairy changed from
The footmen once were lizards
  green,
The coachman once a rat.

Now having danced with the
  prince,
He led her to her place,
While all the ladies at the ball
  Envied her handsome face;
Behold the clock now striking
  twelve,
  Out Cinderella run,
And happily got out of door
  Just as the clock had done.

But in her haste to get away,
  One of her slippers fell,
Which the young prince him-
  self pick'd up,
  And it pleased him so well,
That straight he offer'd a re-
  ward,
  It was ten thousand pound,
To any person that could tell
  Where the owner could be
  found.

And now the sisters tried in
  vain
  The slipper to get on;
Said Cinderella, let me try,
  Dear sisters, when you've
  done; (ease
She tried, and on it went with
  To the foot of Cinderella,
Said She, I think the slipper's
  mine,
  See here I've got the fellow.

THE CHILD'S NEW YEAR'S GIFT.

A pair of Spectacles.

Without a bridle or a saddle,
  Across a thing I ride and straddle.
And those I ride by help of me,
  Tho' almost blind are made to see.

A pair of Stays.

My legs I can venture,
  To say within bound,
Are twelve, if not more,
  Tho' they ne'er touch the ground;
If you search for my eyes,
  More than thirty you'll find
And strange to be told
  They are always behind.

A Pin.

And tho' I'm a brazen-fac'd sharper at best,
No lady without my aid can be drest,
When I'm wanted, Im dragg'd by the head to my duty
And am doomed to be slave to the dress of a beauty.

A letter M.

I'm found in most countries,
  Yet not in earth or sea,
I am in all timber,
  Yet not in any tree,
I am in all metals,
  Yet, as I am told,
I am not in iron, lead,
  Brass, silver, nor gold.

A Pair of Snuffers.

A mouth I have got, that's not whiter than ink.
And all I devour doth most nauseously stink;
So much valued am I, that by none I'm refused,
And the light shines the brighter whenever I'm used.

A Wheelbarrow.

No mouth, no eyes, nor yet a nose,
Two arms two feet, and as it goes,
The feet don't touch the ground,
But all the way the head runs round.

And tho' I can both speak and go alone,
Yet are my motions to myself (unknown.

A Watch.

My form is beauteous to allure the sight
My habit gay, of colour gold & (white,
When ladies take the air, it is my pride,
To walk with equal paces by (their side,
I near their persons constantly remain,
A favourite slave, bound in a (golden chain

A Salamander.

What all consumes best pleases me,
I covet that which others flee,
Strange thing to tell, unhurt I lie
And live, where all the world would die.

Printed by A. Ryle & Paul.

THE GOOD CHILD'S ILLUSTRATED ALPHABET
OR FIRST BOOK.

LONDON:
Published by RYLE & PAUL,
2 & 3, Monmouth Court, Seven Dials.

Was an Archer,
Who shot at a frog.

Was a Butcher,
And kept a great dog.

Was a Captain,
All covered with lace.

Was a Drunkard
And had a red face.

Was an Esquire,
With insolent brow.

Was a Farmer, And
Followed the plough.

Was a Gamester,
Who had but ill-luck.

Was a Huntsman,
And hunted a buck.

Was an Inn-keeper,
Who loved to bouse.

Was a Miser,
And hoarded up gold.

Was a Joiner,
And built up a house.

Was a Nobleman,
Gallant and bold.

Was King William,
Once governed this land.

Was an Oyster-wench,
And went about town.

Was a Lady, who
Had a white hand

Was a Parson, and
Wore a black gown.

Was a Queen,
Who was fond of flip.

Was a Usurer,
A miserly elf.

Was a Robber,
And wanted a whip.

Was a Vinter, who
Drank all himself.

Was a Sailor,
Who spent all he got.

Was a Watchman,
And gaurded the door.

Was a Tinker,
And mended a pot.

Was Expensive,
And so became poor.

Was a Youth,
Who did not love school.

Was a Zany,
A silly old fool.

THE ALPHABET.
The Letters promiscuously arranged.

D B C F G E H A X U Y M V
W N K P J O Z Q I S L T R

z w x o c l y b b f p s m q n v h
k r t g e j a u i

Double and Triple Letters.
ﬁ ﬂ ﬀ ﬃ ﬄ

fi fl fff ffi fl

Diphthongs, &c.
AE Œ æ œ & &c.
Æ OE ae oe and *et* *eœtera*

Arabic Numerals.
1 2 3 4 5 6 7 8 9 0

Roman Numerals.
I. II. III. IV. V. VI. VII. VIII. IX.
X. XI. XII. XIII. XIV.

THE LIFE AND ADVENTURES OF DICK TURPIN.

London: W. S. FORTEY, PRINTER & PUBLISHER,
MONMOUTH COURT, BLOOMSBURY, W.C.

THE
LIFE AND ADVENTURES
OF
DICK TURPIN.

RICHARD TURPIN was born at Hempstead, in Essex, where his father kept the sign of the Bell; and after being the usual time at school, he was bound apprentice to a butcher in Whitechapel, but did not serve out his time, for his master discharged him for impropriety of conduct, which was not in the least diminished by his parents' indulgence in supplying him with money, which enabled him to cut a figure round the town, among the blades of the road and the turf, whose company he usually kept.

His friends, thinking that marriage would reclaim him, persuaded him to marry, which he did with one Hester Palmer, of East Ham in Essex, but he had not long been married before he became acquainted with a gang of thieves, whose depredations terrified the whole county of Essex, and the neighbourhood of London. He joined sheep stealing to foot-pad robbery; and was at last obliged to fly from his place of residence for stealing a young heifer, which he killed and cut up for sale.

Soon after, he stole two oxen from one Farmer Giles, of Plaistow, and drove them to a Butcher's slaughtering house, near Waltham Abbey.

He was followed there, but made his escape out of the window of the house where he was, just as they were entering the door.

He now retreated into the Hundreds of Essex, where he found more security: he adopted a new scheme; and that was to rob the smugglers, but he took care not to attack a gang, only solitary travellers, this he did with a colour of justice, for he pretended to have a deputation from the Customs, and demanded their property in the king's name.

He again joined the gang with whom he had before connected himself, the principal part of those depredations were committed upon Epping Forest, &c.

But this soon becoming an object of magisterial enquiry, he again returned to the solitude of the country, with some more of the gang, and they became notorious deer-stealers, and Turpin being a good shot, sent many a buck up to his connections in London.

DICK TURPIN. 3

They next determined to commence house-breakers; and in this they were much encouraged by joining with Gregory's gang, as it was then called, a company of desparadoes that made the Essex and adjacent roads very dangerous to travel.

Somehow or other, Turpin became acquainted with the circumstances of an old woman, that lived at Laughton, that kept a great quantity of cash by her; whereupon they agreed to rob her; and when they came to the door, Wheeler knocked and Turpin and the rest forcing their way into the house, blindfolded the eyes of the old woman and her maid, and tied the legs of her son to the bedstead, but not finding the wished-for booty, they held a consultation, as they were certain she must have a considerable sum concealed. Turpin told her he knew she had money, and it was in vain to deny it, for have it they would. The old lady persisted that she had none, but Turpin insisting she had money, he swore he would put her on the fire. She continued obstinate and endured for some time, when they took her off the grate, and robbed her of all they could find, upwards of four hundred pounds.

They next proceeded into Surrey, where Turpin and his company robbed Mr. Sheldon's house, near Croydon Church, where they arrived about seven o'clock in the evening. They secured the coachman in the stable. His master hearing some strange voices in the yard, was proceeding to know the cause, when he was met by Turpin, who seizing hold of him compelled him to show them the way into the house, when he secured the door, and confined the rest of the **family in** one room, here they found but little plate and no cash. From **Mr.** Sheldon's person they took eleven guineas, two of which Turpin returned him, begged pardon for what they had done, and wished him a good night.

These robberies hitherto had been carried on entirely on foot, with only the occasional assistance of a hackney coach but now they aspired to appear on horse-back, for which purpose they hired horses at the Old Leaping Bar in Holborn, from whence they set out about two o'clock in the afternoon, and arrived at the Queen's Head, Stanmore, where they staid to regale themselves. It was by this means that Wood, the master of the horse, had so good an opportunity of observing the horses, as to remember the same again when he saw them afterwards in Bloomsbury, where they were taken. About five they went from Mr. Wood's to Stanmore and staid from six until seven and then went together for Mr. Lawrence's, about a mile from thence, where they got about half-past seven. On their arrival at Mr. Lawrence's they alighted from their horses at the gate; whereupon Fielder knocked at the door, and calling out Mr. Lawrence. The man servant thinking it to be some of the neighbours, opened the door, upon which they all rushed **in** with pistols, and seizing Mr.

THE HISTORY OF

DICK TURPIN

Lawrence and his man, threw a cloth over their faces then fell to rifling their pockets, out of which they took one guinea, and about fifteen shillings in silver, with his keys. They said they must have more, and drove Mr. Lawrence up stairs, where coming to a closet, they broke open the door, and took out from thence two guineas, ten shillings a silver cup, 13 silver spoons, and two gold rings. They then rifled the house of all they could get, linen, table cloths, shirts, and the sheets off the bed, and trod the beds under feet, to discover if any money was concealed therein. Suspecting there was more money in the house, they then brought Mr. Lawrence down again, and threatened to cut his throat, and Fielder put a knife to it, as though he intended to do it; to make him confess what money was in the house. One of them took a chopping bill, and threatened to cut off his leg; they then broke his head with their pistols, and dragged him about by the hair of his head. Another of them took the kettle off the fire, and flung it upon him; but it did no other harm just wetting him, because the maid had just before taken out the greater part of the boiling water, and filled it again with cold. After this they dragged him about again, swearing they would "do for him" if he did not immediately inform them where the rest of the money was hid. They then proceeded to make a further search; and then withdrew; threatening to return again in half an hour, and kill every one

DICK TURPIN.   5

they found loose. So saying **they locked them in the** parlour and threw the keys down the area.

Turpin by this robbery got but little, for out of the 26*l*, they took in the whole, he distributed it among them all but three guineas and six shillings and six pence.

A proclamation was issued for the apprehension of the offenders, and a pardon and 50*l* was offered to any of the party who would impeach his accomplices, which however, had no effect. The white Hart in Drury-lane was their place of rendezvous. Here they planned their nightly visits, and here they divided their spoil, and spent the money they acquired.

The robbery being stated to the officers of Westminster, Turpin set off to Alton, where he met with an odd encounter, which got him the best companion he ever had, as he often declared. King, the highwayman, as he was returning from this place to London, being well dressed and mounted, Turpin seeing him have the appearance of a substantial gentleman, rode up to him, and thinking him a fair mark, bid him stand and deliver, and therewith producing his pistols, King fell a laughing at him, and said "what dog rob dog! Come, come, brother Turpin, if you don't know me, I know you, and shall be glad of your company." After a mutual communication of circumstances to each other, they agreed to keep company, and divide good or ill fortune as the trumps might turn up. In fact King was true to him to the last, which was for more than three years.

They met with various fortunes; but being too well known to

2 F

remain long in one place, and as no house that knew them would receive them in it, they formed the resolution of making themselves a cave, covered with bevins and earth, and for that purpose pitched upon a convenient place, enclosed with a thicket, situated on the Waltham side of Epping, near the sign of the King's Oak.

In this place Turpin lived, ate, drank, and lay, for the space of six years, during the first three of which he was enlivened by the drollery of his companion, Tom King, who was a fellow of infinite humour in telling stories, and of an unshaken resolution in attack or defence.

One day, as they were spying from their cave, they discovered a gentleman riding by, that King knew very well to be a rich merchant near Gresham College. This gentleman was in his chariot, and wife with him; his name was Bradele. King first attacked him on the Laughton road; but he being a man of great spirit, offered to make resistance, thinking there was but one; upon which King called Turpin, and bid him hold the horses' heads. They proceeded first to take his money, which he readily parted with, but demurred a good while about his watch, being the dying bequest of his father. King was insisting to take it away, when Turpin interposed, and said, they were more gentlemen than to deprive anyone of their friend's respect which they wore about them, and bid King desist from his demand.

On the day after this transaction they went to the Red Lion ale house, in Aldersgate street, where they had not been more than half an hour, when Turpin heard of the approach of the chief constable and his party; they mounted each their horse; but before King could get fairly seated he was seized by one of the party, and called on Dick to fire. Turpin replied, "If I do, I shall hit you." "Fire, if you are my friend." said King—Turpin fired, but the ill-fated ball took effect in King's breast. Dick stood a moment in grief, but self-preservation made him urge his mare forward to elude his pursuers; it was now he resolved on a journey to York, and raising himself in his saddle, he said, "By G—, I will do it." Encouraged by "Hark-away Bess," she flew on.

Astonishing to relate, he reached York the same evening and was noticed playing at bowls in the bowling-green with several gentlemen there, which circumstance saved him from the hands of justice for a time. His pursuers coming up and seeing Turpin, knew him; and caused him to be taken into custody; one of them swore to him and the horse he rode on, which was the identical one he arrived upon in that city; but on being in the stable, and its rider at play, and all in the space of four-and-twenty hours, his alibi was admitted; for the magistrates of York could not believe it possible for one horse to cover the ground, being upwards of 190 miles, in so short a space.

DICK TURPIN. 7

For the last two years of his life he seems to have confined his residence to the county of York, where he appears to be a little known. He often accompanied the neighbouring gentlemen in their parties of hunting and shooting; and one evening, on a return from an expedition of the latter kind, he saw one of his landlord's cocks in the street, which he shot.

The next day Mr. Hall received a letter from Robert Appleton, Long Sutton, with this account :—that the said John Palmer had lived there about three quarters of a year, and had before that been once apprehended, and made his escape, and that they had a strong suspicion he was guilty of horse-stealing.

Another information gave notice, that he had stolen a horse from Captain Dawson, of Ferraby; his horse was that which Turpin rode on when he came to Beverley, and which he stole from off Hickinton Fen in Lincolnshire.

He wrote to his father upon being convicted, to use his interest to get him off for transportation, but his fate was at hand, his notoriety caused application to be ineffectual.

After he had been in prison five months, he was removed from Beverley to York Castle to take his trial. When on his trial his case seemed much to affect the hearers. He had two trials, upon both of which he was convicted upon the fullest evidence. After a long trial the Jury brought in their Verdict and found him Guilty.

He was carried in a cart to the place of execution, on Saturday, April, 7th, 1739. He behaved himself with amazing assurance and bowed to the spectators as he passed. It was remarkable that as he mounted the ladder, his right leg trembled, on which he stamped it down with an air, 'and with undaunted courage looked round about him; and after speaking near half an hour to the topman, threw himself off the ladder, and expired in about five minutes.

W. S. Fortey, Printer, Monmouth Court, Bloomsbury.

"THE CATNACH PRESS,"

(ESTABLISHED 1813.)

WILLIAM S. FORTEY,

(Sole Successor to the late J. Catnach.)

Printer, Publisher,

AND

WHOLESALE STATIONER,
2 & 3, MONMOUTH COURT,
SEVEN DIALS, LONDON, W.C.

The Cheapest and Greatest Variety in the Trade of Large Coloured Penny Books; Halfpenny Coloured Books; Farthing Books; Penny and Halfpenny Panoramas; School Books; Penny and Halfpenny Song Books; Memorandum Books; **Poetry** Cards; Lotteries; Ballads (4000) and **Hymns**; Valentines, Scripture Sheets; Christmas Pieces; Twelfth Night Characters, Carols; Book and Sheet Almanacks, Envelopes, Note Paper, &c.

W. S. **FORTEY** begs to inform his Friends and the Public generally, that after 19 years service he has succeeded to the business of his late employers (A. Ryle & Co.), and intends carrying on the same, trusting that his long experience will be a recommendation, and that no exertion shall be wanting on his part to merit a continuance of those favours that have been so liberally bestowed on that Establishment during the last 46 years.

1859

THE LONG SONG-SELLER.

SONGS AND SONG LITERATURE.

"Old songs, old songs—what heaps I knew,
From 'Chevy Chase' to 'Black-eyed Sue';
From 'Flow, thou regal, purple stream,'
To 'Rousseau's melancholy 'Dream!'
I loved the pensive 'Cabin Boy,'
With earnest truth and real joy.
To greet 'Tom Bowling' and 'Poor Jack';
And, oh! 'Will Watch,' the 'Smuggler' bold,
My plighted troth thou'lt ever hold."

ELIZA COOK.

"Songs! Songs! Songs! Beautiful songs! Love songs! Newest songs! Old songs! Popular songs! Songs, *Three Yards a Penny!*" was a "standing dish" at the "Catnach Press," and Catnach was the Leo X. of street publishers. And it is said that he at one time kept a fiddler on the premises, and that he used to sit receiving ballad-writers and singers, and judging of the merits of any production which was brought to him, by having it sung then and there to some popular air played by his own fiddler, and so that the ballad-singer should be enabled to start at once, not only with the new song, but also the tune to which it was adapted. His broad-sheets contain all sorts of songs and ballads, for he had a most catholic taste, and introduced the custom of taking from any writer, living or dead, whatever he fancied, and printing it side by side with the productions of his own clients.

He naturally had a bit of a taste for old ballads, music, and song writing; and in this respect he was far in advance of many of his contemporaries. To bring within the reach of all the standard and popular works of the day, had been the ambition of the elder Catnach; whilst the son was, *nolens volens*, incessant in his endeavours in trying to promulgate and advance, not the beauty, elegance, and harmony which pervades many of our national airs and ballad poetry, but very often the worst and vilest of each and every description—in other words, those most suitable for street-sale. His stock of songs was very like his customers, diversified. There were all kinds, to suit all classes. Love, sentimental, and comic songs were so interwoven as to form a trio of no ordinary amount of novelty. At ordinary times, when the Awfuls and Sensationals were flat, Jemmy did a large stroke of business in this line.

It is said that when the "Songs—*Three-yards-a-penny*"—first came out and had all the attractions of novelty, some men sold twelve or fourteen dozen on fine days during three or four of the summer months, so clearing between 6s. and 7s. a day, but on the average about 25s. a week profit. The "long songs," however, have been quite superseded by the "Monster" and "Giant Penny Song Books." Still there are a vast number of half-penny ballad-sheets worked off, and in proportion to their size, far more than the "Monsters" or "Giants."

As a rule there are but two songs printed on the half-penny ballad-sheets—generally a new and popular song with another older ditty, or a comic and sentimental, and "adorned" with two woodcuts. These are selected without any regard as to their fitness to the subject, and in most cases have not the slightest reference to the ballad of which they form the head-piece. For instance :—"The Heart that can feel for another" is illustrated by a gaunt and savage looking lion ; "When I was first Breeched," by an engraving of a Highlander *sans culotte;* "The Poacher" comes under the cut of a youth with a large watering-pot, tending flowers ; "Ben Block" is heralded by the rising sun; "The London Oyster Girl," by Sir Walter Raleigh ; "The Sailor's Grave," by the figure of Justice ; "Alice Grey" comes under the very dilapidated figure of a sailor, or "Jolly Young Waterman ;" "Bright Hours are in store for us yet" is *headed* with a *tail-piece* of an urn, on which is inscribed FINIS ! "The Wild Boar Hunt," by two wolves chasing a deer ; "The Dying Child to its Mother," by an Angel appearing to an old man ; "Autumn Leaves lie strew'd around," by a ship in full sail ; "Cherry Ripe," by Death's Head and Cross Bones ; Jack at the Windlass," falls under a Roadside Inn ; while "William Tell" is presented to the British public in form and style of an old woman nursing an infant of squally nature. Here follow a few examples of the style, also that of some of the ballad-sheets : together with various *verbatim* imprints used by "THE CATNACH PRESS," chronologically arranged from *circa* 1813 to the present time.

THE GALLANT SAILOR.

London:
Printed by J. Catnach, and sold Wholesale and Retail at
No. 60, Wardour Street, Soho Square.

Farewell thou dear and Gallant Sailor,
  Since thou and I have parted been,
Be thou constant and true hearted,
  And I will be the same to thee.

CHORUS.
May the winds and waves direct thee,
  To some wishful port design'd,
If you love me, don't deceive me,
  But let your heart be as true as mine.

*   *   *   *   *   *

When oft times my fancy tells me,
  That in battle thou art slain,
With true love I will requite thee,
When thou dost return again.
          May the winds, &c.

O RARE TURPIN.

Printed by J. Catnach, 2, Monmouth Court, 7 Dials.
Sold by J. Sharman, Cambridge, Bennet, Brighton; & R. Harris, Salisbury.

As I was riding over Hunslow Moor,
There I saw a lawyer riding before,
And I asked him if he was not afraid,
To meet bold Turpin that mischievous blade.
CHORUS.—I asked him if he was not afraid,
To meet bold Turpin that mischievous blade.
Says Turpin to the lawyer and for to be cute,
My money I have hid all in my boot,
Says the lawyer to Turpin they mine can't find,
For I have hid mine in the cape of my coat behind.
I rode till I came to a powder mill,
Where Turpin bid the lawyer for to stand still,
For the cape of your coat it must come off,
For my horse is in want of a new saddle cloth.
Now Turpin robbed the lawyer of all his store,
When that's gone he knows where to get more,
And the very next town that you go in,
Tell them you was robb'd by the bold Turpin.

THE HISTORY OF

MOUNTAIN MAID.

Printed by J. Catnach, 2, Monmouth Court, 7 Dials.
Travellers and Shopkeepers supplied with Sheet Hymns. Patters, and Slip Songs as Cheap and Good as any Shop in London.

The Mountain Maid from her bower has hied,
And speed to the glassy river's side,
Where the radiant mead shone clear and bright,
And the willows wav'd in the silver light.
On a mossy bank lay a shepherd swain,
He woke his pipe to tuneful strain,
And so blythely gay were the notes he play'd,
That he charm'd the ear of the Mountain Maid.

She step'd with timid fear oppress'd,
While soft sighs swell her gentle breast,
He caught her glance, and mark'd her sigh,
And triumph laugh'd in his sparkling eye.
So softly sweet was the tuneful ditty,
He charmed her tender heart to pity ;
And so blithely gay were the notes he play'd,
That he gain'd the heart of the Mountain Maid.

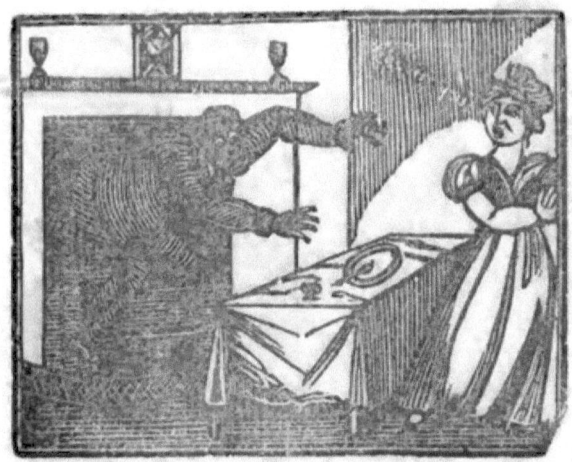

MEET ME IN THE WILLOW GLEN

J. Catnach, Printer, 2, Monmouth Court, 7 Dials. Cards, &c. Printed Cheap. ☞ Country Shops and Travellers supplied.

Meet me in the willow glen,
   Where the silvery moon is beaming,
Songs of love I'll sing thee then,
   When all the world is dreaming.

Meet me in the willow glen.
   When the silver moon is beaming,
Songs of love I'll sing thee then,
   If you meet me in the willow glen.

No prying eye shall come love.
   No stranger foot be seen.
And the busy village hum, love,
   Shall echo through the glen.
             Meet me, &c.

THE HISTORY OF

DRINK TO ME ONLY WITH THINE EYES.

J. Catnach, Printer, 2, Monmouth Court, 7 Dials.   Sold by W. Marshall.
Sold by T. Pierce, Southborough.   (Cards Printed Cheap.)

Drink to me only with thine eyes,
   And I will pledge with mine,
Or leave a kiss but in the cup,
   And I'll not look for wine;
The thirst that from my soul doth rise,
   Doth ask a drink divine;
But might I of Jove's nectar sip,
   I would not change for thine.

The Mistletoe Bough.

Printed by by J. Catnach, 2, Monmouth Court, 7 Dials. Sold by Pierce, Southborough, Bennet, Brighton; and Sharman, Cambridge.

The mistletoe hung in the castle hall,
The holly branch shone on the old oak wall,
The baron's retainers were blithe and gay,
And keeping their Christmas holiday.
The baron beheld with a father's pride,
His beautiful child, young Lovell's bride:
While she with her bright eyes, seemed to be
The star of the goodly company.
     Oh! the mistletoe bough!

"I'm weary of dancing now," she cried!
"Here tarry a moment—I'll hide—I'll hide,
And, Lovell, be sure thou'rt the first to trace
The clue to my secret lurking place."
Away she ran—and her friends began
Each tower to search, and each nook to scan;
And young Lovell cried, "Oh! where dost thou hide?
I'm lonesome without thee, my own dear bride."
     Oh! the mistletoe bough!

THE HISTORY OF

THE
Rose will Cease to Blow.

Printed by J. Catnach, 2, Monmouth Court, 7 Dials. Sold by T. Batchelor, 14, Hackney Road Crescent; W. Marshall, Bristol. Sold by Bennet and Boyes, Brighton.

The rose will cease to blow,
  The eagle turn a dove,
The streams will cease to flow,
  Ere I will cease to love.

The sun shall cease to shine,
  The world shall cease to move,
The stars their light resign,
  Ere I will cease to love.

I'M A TOUGH
True Hearted Sailor.

J. Catnach, Printer, 2 & 3, Monmouth Court, 7 Dials, & at 14, Waterloo Road, (late Hill's). Country Shops, and Travellers supplied.

I'm a tough true-hearted sailor,
   Careless and all that, d'ye see,
Never at the times a railer—
   What is time or tide to me?
All must die when fate must will it,
   Providence ordains it so;
Every bullet has its billet,
   Man the boat, boys—Yeo, heave, yeo!

Life's at best a sea of trouble,
   He who fears it is a dunce,
Death, to me, an empty bubble,
   I can never die but once,
Blood, if duty bids, I'll spill it,
   Yet I have a tear for woe,
      Every bullet has its billet, &c.

THE HISTORY OF

WHEN BIBO THOUGHT FIT.

Printed and Sold by J. CATNACH, 2 & 3, Monmouth Court, 7 Dials.

When Bibo thought fit from the world to retreat,
As full of champagne as an egg's full of meat;
He wak'd in the boat, and to Charon he said,
He would be rowed back, for he was not yet dead.
'Trim the boat, and sit quiet, stern Charon replied—
'You may have forgot—you were drunk when you died!'

THE
SUN
That Lights the ROSES.

A. Ryle and Co., Printers, 2 & 3, Monmouth Court, Seven Dials, and 35, Hanover Street, Portsea, where upwards of 4000 different sorts of ballads are continually on sale together with 40 new penny song books.

Tho' dimple cheeks may give delight
  Where rival beauties blossom;
Th'o balmy lips to love invite,
  To extacy the bosom.
Yet sweeter far yon summer sky,
  Whose blushing tints discloses,
Give me the lustre beaming eye,
  The Sun that lights the Roses.

THE HISTORY OF

THE
Woodpecker.

London :—Printed by J. Paul & Co., 2 & 3, Monmouth Court.

I knew by the smoke that so gracefully curl'd
  Above the green elms, that a cottage was near,
And I said if there's peace to be found it the world,
  A heart that is humble might hope for it here.
CHORUS.
Every leaf was at rest, and I heard not a sound,
But the woodpecker tapping in the hollow beech tree.

And here in this lone little wood, I exclaim'd,
  With a maid who was lovely to soul and to eye,
Who would blush when I prais'd her, and weep if I blam'd,
  How blest could I live, and how calm could I die.
                        Every leaf, &c.

YE
Topers All.

London :—Published by Ryle and Paul, 2 & 3, Monmouh Court, 7 Dials. Where an immense number of songs are always ready.

Ye topers all drink to the soul,
   Of this right honest fellow;
Who always loved a flowing bowl,
   And would in death be mellow.
The lamp of life be kindled up,
   With spirit stout and glowing;
His heart inspired thus with a cup,
   Ascends where nectar's flowing.

Death of Nelson.

London:—Ryle & Co., Printers, 2 & 3, Monmouth Court, Bloomsbury.

RECITATIVE.

O'er Nelson's tomb, with silent grief oppress'd
Britannia mourns her hero now at rest.
But these bright laurels ne'er shall fade with years,
Whose leaves are water'd by a Nation's tears.

AIR.

'Twas in Trafalgar's bay,
We saw the Frenchmen lay,
   Each heart was bounding then;
We scorned the foreign yoke—
Our ships were British oak,
   And hearts of oak our men,
Our Nelson mark'd them on the wave,
Three cheers our gallant seamen gave,
   Nor thought of home or beauty;
Along the line this signal ran—
England expects that every man
   This day will do his duty!"

THE SCARLET FLOWER.

A. Ryle & Co., Printers, 2 & 3, Monmouth Court, Bloomsbury.

She's gentle as the zephyr,
  That sips of every sweet,
She fairer than the fairest lily,
  In nature's soft retreat;
Her eyes are like the crystal brok,
  As bright and clear to see?
Her lips outshine the Scarlet Flow'r
  Of bonny Ellerslie.

THE HISTORY OF

THE THORN.

London :—Printed at the "Catnach Press" by W. Fortey, (late A. Ryle) 2 & 3, Monmouth Court. Bloomsbury. (Established 1813.) The Oldest and Cheapest House in the World for Ballads, (4,000 sorts) Song Books, &c.

From the white blossomed sloe,
   My dear Chloe requested,
A sprig her fair breast to adorn;
   No by heavens I exclaimed, may I perish
If ever I plant in that bosom a thorn.

When I shewed her the ring and implored her to marry
   She blushed like the dawning of morn,
Yes I'll consent she replyed if you'll promise,
   That no jealous rival shall laugh me to scorn,
No by heavens I exclaim'd may I perish,
   If ever I plant in that bosom a thorn.

BANKS
OF THE NILE.

Printed at the "Catnach Press" by W. FORTEY, Monmouth Court, Bloomsbury, the Oldest House in the World for Ballads (4,000 sorts) Song Books, &c. &c.

Hark! I hear the drums a beating—no longer can I stay,
I hear the trumpets sounding, my love I must away,
We are ordered from Portsmouth many a long mile,
For to join the British soldiers on the banks of the Nile.

Willie, dearest Willie, don't leave me here to mourn,
You'll make me curse and rue the day that ever I was born,
For the parting of my own true love is parting of my life,
So stay at home dear Willie, and I will be your wife.

I will cut off my yellow locks, and go along with you,
I will dress myself in velveteens, and go see Egypt too
I will fight or bear your banner, while kind fortune seems to smile,
And we'll comfort one another on the banks of the Nile.

THE HISTORY OF
Poor Crazy JANE.

London :—Printed at the "Catnach Press" by W. S. Fortey, 2 & 3, Monmouth Court, Bloomsbury. (Established 1813.) The Oldest and Cheapest House in the World for Ballads, Song Books, Children's Spelling & Reading Books, Panorama Slips, Almanacks, Valentines, Hymns, Toy Cards, Poetry Cards, Lotteries, Characters, Note Paper, Envelopes, &c.
*** Shopkeepers and Hawkers supplied on the lowest terms.

Why fair maid in every feature,
    Are such signs of fear expressed,
Can a wandering wretched creature,
    With such horror fill thy breast.
Do my frenzied looks alarm thee,
    Trust me, sweet, thy fears are vain,
Not for Kingdom would I harm thee,
    Shun not then poor crazy Jane.

Fondly my young heart believed him,
    Which was doomed to love but one ;
He sighed, he vowed, and I believed him,
    He was false, and I'm undone.
From that hour has reason never,
    Had her empire o'er my brain,
Henry fled, with him for ever
    Fled the wits of Crazy Jane.

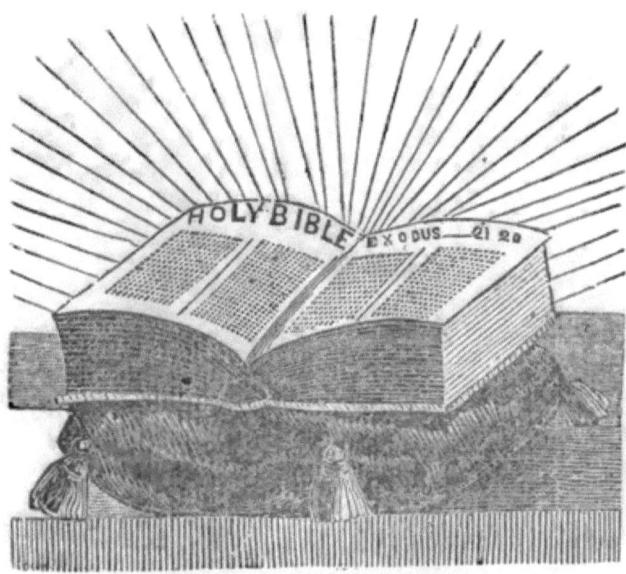

"It was Christmas morning—dear Christmas morning
When bright angels and men kept watch for its dawning—
And merrily Christmas bells were out ringing,
And blithely the children their carols were singing—
'Twas a hundred years agone—or more."

From time immemorial the ballad singer, with his rough and ready broad-sheet, has travelled over the whole surface of the country in all seasons and weathers, yet there was one time of the year, however, when he went out of his every-day path and touched on deeper matters than accidents, politics, prize fights, sporting matches, murders, battles, royalty, famous men and women. Christmas time brought, both to him and his audience, its witness of the unity of the great family of heaven and earth, its story of the life and death of Him in whom that unity stands.

Several examples, of Christmas carols and Scripture-sheets, bearing Catnach's imprint lie before us, thanks to the kindness of Mr. W. S. Fortey, Catnach's successor; these broadsides bear several distinctive marks which show that it was an object of more than ordinary care to publishers and ballad singers. In the first place, these Christmas sheets are double the size of the ordinary broad-sheet—measuring 30 inches by 20—and contain four or five carols—generally one long narrative ballad, and three or four short pieces. Each of them having two or three large woodcuts and several of smaller sizes, and having the following distinctive titles—The **Trial of Christ**. **Faith, Hope, and Charity**. **Our Saviour's Love**. **The Tree of Life**. **The Crucifixion**. **The Saviour of Mankind**. **The Messiah**. **The Harp of Israel**. **The Saviour's Garland**. **Divine Mirth**. And **The Life of Joseph**, to which is appended :—

LONDON: PRINTED AND SOLD BY
J. CATNACH, 2, MONMOUTH COURT, 7, DIALS,
WHERE MAY BE HAD THE FOLLOWING SHEETS, WITH CUTS.

The Last Day, Our Saviour's Letter, The Son of Righteousness, Travels of the Children of Israel, Glory of. Solomon, The Morning Star, The Noble Army of Martyrs, Christmas Gambols, The Hertfordshire Tragedy, and a Variety of Others are in a state of forwardness for the Press.

"Looking at these Christmas broad-sheets," says the writer of an article on street-ballads, in the "National Review," for October, 1861, "it would really seem as if the poorest of our brethren claimed their right to higher nourishment than common for their minds and souls, as well as for their bodies, at the time of year when all Christendom should rejoice. And this first impression is confirmed when we examine their contents. In all those which we have seen, the only piece familiar to us is that noble old carol 'While shepherds watched their flocks by night,' where the rest come from, we cannot even conjecture ; but in the whole of them there is not one which we should wish were not there. We have been unable to detect in them even a coarse expression ; and of the hateful narrowness and intolerance, the namby-pamby, the meaningless cant, the undue familiarity with holy things, which makes us turn with a shudder from so many modern collections of hymns, there is simply nothing.

"Account for it how we will, there is the simple fact. Perhaps it may lead us to think somewhat differently of those whom we are in the habit of setting down in the mass as little better than heathens. We cannot conclude this article better than by giving an extract or two from these Christmas broad-sheets."

"The Saviour's Garland, a choice Collection of the most esteemed Carols," has the usual long narrative ballad, which begins:

"Come, all you faithful Christians
    That dwell upon the earth,—
Come celebrate the morning
    Of our dear Saviour's birth:
This is the happy morning,—
    This is the happy morn
Whereon, to save our ruined race,
    The Son of God was born."

And after telling simply the well-known story, it ends:
"Now to him up ascended,
    Then let your praises be,
That we His steps may follow,
    And He our pattern be;
That when our lives are ended
    We may hear His blessed call:
'Come, Souls, receive the Kingdom
    Prepared for you all.'"

Another, "The Star of Bethlehem, a collection of esteemed Carols for the present year," opens its narrative thus:

"Let all that are to mirth inclined
Consider well and bear in mind
What our good God for us has done,
In sending His beloved Son.

Let all our songs and praises be
Unto His heavenly Majesty;
And evermore amongst our mirth
Remember Christ our Saviour's birth.

The twenty-fifth day of December
We have great reason to remember;
In Bethlehem, upon that morn,
There was a blessed Saviour born," &c.

One of the short pieces, by no means the best, we give whole :

> "With one consent let all the earth
>   The praise of God proclaim,
> Who sent the Saviour, by whose birth
>   To man salvation came.
>
> All nations join and magnify
>   The great and wondrous love
> Of Him who left for us the sky,
>   And all the joys above.
>
> But vainly thus in hymns of praise
>   We bear a joyful part,
> If while our voices loud we raise,
>   We lift not up our heart.
>
> We, by a holy life alone,
>   Our Saviour's laws fulfil ;
> By those His glory is best shown
>   Who best perform His will.
>
> May we to all His words attend
>   With humble, pious care ;
> Then shall our praise to heaven ascend,
>   And find acceptance there."

We do not suppose that the contents of these Christmas broadsheets are supplied by the same persons who write the murderballads, or the attacks on crinoline. They may be borrowed from well known hymn books for anything we know. But if they are borrowed, we must still think it much to the credit of the selectors, that, where they might have found so much that is objectionable and offensive, they should have chosen as they have done. We only hope that their successors, whoever they may be who will become the caterers for their audiences, will set nothing worse before them.

Christmas broad-sheets formed an important item in the office of the "Catnach Press," as the sale was enormous, and Catnach always looked forward for a large return of capital, and a "good clearance" immediately following the spurt for Guy Fawkes' speeches, in October of each year. But although the sale was very large, it only occupies one "short month." This enabled them to make Carols a stock job, so that when trade in the Ballad, Sensational, "Gallows," or any other line of business was dull, they used to fill up every spare hour in the working off or colouring them, so as to be ready to meet the extraordinary demand which was sure to be made at the fall of the year.

Like most of the old English customs, Christmas-carol singing is fast dying out. Old peripatetic stationers well remember the rich harvest they once obtained at Christmas times by carol selling. Now there are very few who care to invest more than a shilling or two at a time on the venture; whereas in times long past, all available capital was readily embarked in the highly-coloured and plain sheets of the birth of our Saviour, with the carol of "Christians awake," or "The Seven Good Joys of Mary:"—

"The first good joy our Mary had,
　　It was the joy of one,
To see her own Son, Jesus,
　　To suck at her breast-bone.
To suck at her breast-bone, God-man,
　　And blessed may He be,
Both Father, Son, and Holy Ghost,
　　To all eternity."

Now, whether carol singing has degenerated with carol poetry, and consequently the sale of Christmas carols diminished is a question we need not enter upon; but when we turn to the fine old carols of our forefathers, we cannot help regretting that many of these are buried in the records of the long past.

Here are a couple of verses of one, said to be the first carol or drinking-song composed in England. The original is in Anglo-Norman French:—

"Lordlings, from a distant home,
  To seek old Christmas are we come,
    Who loves our minstrelsy—
And here unless report mis-say,
The greybeard dwells; and on this day
Keeps yearly wassail, ever gay
    With festive mirth and glee.

  * * * * * *

Lordlings, it is our host's command,
And Christmas joins him hand in hand,
    To drain the brimming bowl;
And I'll be foremost to obey,
Then pledge we, sirs, and drink away,
For Christmas revels here to day,
    And sways without control.

Now *wassail* to you all! and merry may you be,
And foul that wight befall, who drinks not health to me."

One can well imagine the hearty feeling which would greet a party of minstrels carolling out such a song as the above in Christmas days of yore; and then contrast the picture with a *troupe* from St. Giles's or Whitechapel bawling out "God Rest you Merry Gentlemen!" The very thought of the contrast sends a shudder through the whole human system; and no wonder the first were received with welcome feasting, and the latter driven "with more kicks than half-pence" from the doors.

In an old book of "Christmasse Carolles newely emprinted at London, in the fletestrete at the sygne of the Sonne by Wynkyn de Worde. The yere of our Lorde, m.d.xxi. Quarto." Is a carol on "Bryngyng in the Bore's Head":—

"The bore's head in hand bring I,
  With garlandes gay and rosemary,
  I pray you all synge merely,
    Qui estis in convivio.

The bore's head, I understande
Is the chiefe servyce in this lande,
Loke wherever it be fande,
  Servite cum Contico.

Be gladde, lordes, both more and lasse,
  For this hath ordayned our stewarde,
  To chere you all this Christmasse
    The bore's head with mustarde.'

252   THE HISTORY OF

With certain alterations, this carol is still, or at least was very recently, retained at Queen's College, Oxford, and sung to a cathedral chant of the psalms.

It would occupy too much space to search into the origin of Christmas carols. They are doubtless coeval with the original celebrations of Christmas, first as a strictly Romish sacred ceremony, and afterwards as one of joyous festivity.

This "Moral-Sheet" entitled "THE STAGES OF LIFE: or, The various Ages and Degrees of Human Life explained by these Twelve different Stages, from our Birth to our Graves," had a great sale.

INFANCY

To 10 Years old.

"HIS vain delusive thoughts are fill'd
　　With vain delusive joys—
The empty bubble of a dream,
　　Which waking change to toys."

From 10 to 20 Years old.

"HIS heart is now puff'd up,
　　He scorns the tutor's hand;
He hates to meet the least control
　　And glories to command."

From 20 to 30 Years old.

"THERE's naught here that can withstand
　　The rage of his desire,
His wanton flames are now blown up,
　　His mind is all on fire."

From 30 to 40 Years old.

"LOOK forward and repent
  Of all thy errors past,
That so thereby thou may'st attain
 True happiness at last."

From 40 to 50 Years old.

"AT fifty years he is
  Like the declining sun,
For now his better half of life,
 Man seemeth to have run."

From 50 to 60 Years old.

"HIS wasted taper now
  Begins to lose its light,
His sparkling flames doth plainly show
 'Tis growing towards night."

From 60 to 70 Years old.

"PERPLEX'D with slavish fear
  And unavailing woe,
He travels on life's rugged way
 With locks as white as snow."

From 70 to 80 Years old.

"INFIRMITY is great,
  At this advanced age,
And ceaseless grief and weakness leagued,
 Now vent their bitter rage."

From 80 to 90 Years old.

"LIFE'S 'Vital Spark'—the soul,
  Is hovering on the verge
Of an eternal world above,
 And waiting to emerge."

From 90 to 100 Years old.

"THE sun is sinking fast
       Behind the clouds of earth,
Oh may it shine with brigher beams,
    Where light receiv'd her birth."

Catnach was now at the height of his fame as a printer of ballads, Christmas-pieces, carols, lotteries, execution papers, dying speeches, catchpennies, primers and battledores, and his stock of type and woodcuts had very considerably increased to meet his business demands. And it may be said that he was the very Napoleon of buyers at sales by auction of "printers' stock." On one occasion, when lot after lot was being knocked down to him, one of the "Littlejohn crew" of "knock-out-men" of the period, observed to the auctioneer, "Why, sir, Mr. Catnach is buying up all the lots." "Yes," replied the auctioneer, "And what's more, Mr. Catnach will pay for them and clear away all his lots in the morning;" then adding somewhat pointedly, "which is a thing I can't say of all parties who attend my sales."

But although we are informed, *vivâ voce* of a contemporary, that Jemmy Catnach was so large a buyer at sales by auction of "printers' stock," we may, with some degree of safety, come to the conclusion that he could have only bought such lots that would be considered by other master printers as worthless, and that it was the apparent cheapness that would be the incentive for his buying up all the worn-out and battered letter, for Jemmy was a man who hated "innowations" as he used to call improvements, and he, therefore, had a great horror in laying out his money in new and improved manufactured type, because, as he observed, he kept so many standing forms, and when certain sorts ran short he was not particular, and would tell the boys to use anything which would make a good shift. For instance, he never considered a compositor could be aground for a lowercase "l" while he had a figure "1" or a cap "I" to fall back upon; by the same rule, the cap. "O" and figure "0" were synonymous with "Jemmy;" the lowercase "p," "b," "d," and "q," would all do duty for each other in *turn*, and if they could not always find Roman letters to finish a word with, why the compositor knew very well that the "reader" would not mark out Ita*lic*, nor wrong founts.

From a small beginner in the world, Catnach was soon able to see his way clear to amass a fortune. He had now established his reputation as a man of enterprise, and he was very sensitive to maintain a sort of shabby-genteel appearance. It was amusing, especially when over his glass, to hear him describe the effect the "awfuls" had on the public. The proprietor of any of our leading journals could not have felt prouder than did Catnach, as he saw drafted from his press the many thousands of varied productions.

We will now briefly allude to the wood-blocks which Catnach had in his possession, and which served for the purpose of illustrating during the time that he had been in business. He had a large collection, such as they were; but as works of art they had little or no pretension, being, upon the whole, of the oddest and most ludicrous character. Those that were intended for the small books were very quaint—as we have shown by the fac-similed specimens we have given—whilst the larger portion, which were chiefly intended for the "awfuls," were grotesque and hideous in their design and execution. No more ghastly sight could be imagined than one of Jemmy's embellishments of an execution. It would appear that for the last discharge of the law he had a large collection of blocks which would suit any number of victims who were about to undergo the dread penalty. It mattered little how many Jack Ketch was going to operate upon, wood-blocks to the exact number were always adopted, in this particular the great "Dying Speech Merchant" would seem to have thought that his honour and reputation were at stake, for he had his network so formed as to be able to secure every information of news that was passing between the friends of the culprits and the prerogative of the Crown. But we are imformed that upon one occasion he was nearly entrapped. Three victims were upon the eve of being executed, and in those days—and in later times—it was not an uncommon thing to see the confession and dying speech printed one or two days previous to the event. This we are told by those in the trade was almost necessary, in order that the sheets might be ready for the provinces almost as soon as the sentence of the law had been carried out. It so happened that on the night previous to an execution, one of the culprits was reprieved. It was solely by a piece of good luck that Catnach heard of it. Several sheets had been struck off; and Jemmy was often chaffed about hanging three men instead of two; but our informant assures us that the error was corrected before any of the impressions were dispatched from the office. Had they gone before the public in their original state, the *locus standi* of the great publisher in Monmouth Court would have been greatly imperilled. To those who are fond of the fine arts, *in usum vulgi*, Catnach's embellishments will afford a fund of amusement. Amongst the lot were several well known places, the scenes of horrible and awful crimes, engravings of debauchery and ill-fame, together with an endless number of different kinds, suitable at the shortest possible notice, to illustrate every conceivable and inconceivable subject.

The Seven Dials in general, and "The Catnach Press" in particular, had no dread of copyright law—the principal Librarian of the British Museum, Stationers', or any other Hall in those days—and as wood engravings were not to be had then so quickly or cheaply as now-a-days, Jemmy used at times to be his own engraver, and while the compositors were setting up the types, he would carve out the illustration on the back of an old pewter music plate, and by nailing it on to a piece of wood make it into an improvised stereo-plate off-hand, for he was very handy at this sort of work, at which also his sister, with his instruction, could assist; so they soon managed to rough out a figure or two, and when things were dull and slack they generally got one or two subjects ready in stock, such as a highwayman with crape over his face, shooting a traveller, who is falling from his horse near a wide-spreading old elm tree, through which the moon was to be seen peeping; not forgetting to put the highwayman in top boots and making him a regular dandy. This was something after the plan of the artists of the cheap illustrated papers of the present day, who generally anticipate events sometime beforehand to be ready with their blocks. As a proof of this, the editor of the "London, Provincial, and Colonial Press News," says "I happened to call one day on an artist for the 'Illustrated Press,' and found him busily engaged in sketching a funeral procession with some twenty coffins borne on the shoulders of men who were winding their way through an immense crowd. Upon inquiry, I was told that it was intended for the next week's issue, and was to represent the the funeral of the victims of the late dreadful colliery explosion, for although the inquest was only then sitting, and all the bodies had not yet been found, there was sure to be a funeral of that kind when it was all over, and as they did not know how many bodies were to be buried at one time, it was very cleverly arranged to commence the procession from the *corner of the block*, and so leave it to the imagination as to how many more coffins were coming in the rear; something after the plan of a small country theatre, when representing Richard the Third, and in the battle scene, after the first two or three of the army had made their appearance, to cry 'halt!' very loudly to all those behind who were not seen, and leave the spectators to guess how many hundreds their were to come.

For the illustrating of catchpennies, broadsides, and street-literature in general, particular kinds of wood-cuts were required. In most cases one block was called upon to perform many parts; and the majority of metropolitan printers, who went in for this work, had only a very limited number of them. Very often the same cuts were repeated over and over again, and made to change sides as one another, and that simply to make a little variation from a ballad or broadside that had been printed at the same office on the day, week, or month previous. It mattered little what the subject was, it required some adornment, in the shape of illustration, to give effect to it. The catchpennies, especially those connected with the awful, were in general very rough productions. A lover strangling his sweetheart with a long piece of rope. A heartless woman murdering an innocent man. Vice punished and virtue rewarded, and similar subjects, were always handled in such a manner as to create a degree of excitement, sympathy, and alarm. The broadsides, generally adorned with some rough outline of the royal arms of England, a crowned king or queen, as the subject might be, received their full share of consideration at the hands of the artist. Scions of royal blood, and those connected with the court, were often painted in colours glaring and attractive, whilst the matter set forth in the letterpress was not always the most flattering or encouraging.

CATCH-PENNY:—Any temporary contrivance to obtain money from the public; penny shows, or cheap exibitions. Also descriptions of murders, fires, and terrible accidents, &c., which have never taken place.

Hotton's: *Slang Dictionary.*

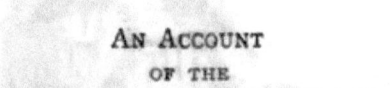

An Account
of the
DREADFUL APPARITION

That appeared last night to Henry ——— in this street, of Mary ———, the shopkeeper's daughter round the corner, in a shroud, all covered in white.

The castle clock struck one—the night was dark, drear, and tempestuous.—Henry sat in an antique chamber of it, over a wood fire, which in the stupor of contemplation, he had suffered to decrease into a few lifeless embers; on the table by him lay the portrait of Mary—the features of which were not very perfectly disclosed by a taper, that just glimmered in the socket. He took up the portrait, however, and gazing intensely upon it, till the taper, suddenly burning brighter, discovered to him a phenomenon he was not less terrified than surprised at.—The eyes of the portrait moved;—the features from an angelic smile, changed to a look of solemn sadness; a tear stole down each cheek, and the bosom palpitated as with sighing.

Again the clock struck *one!*—it had struck the same hour but ten minutes before.—Henry heard the castle gate grate on its hinges—it slammed too—the clock struck one again—and a deadly groan echoed through the castle. Henry was not subject to superstitious fears—neither was he a coward;—yet a hero of romance might have been justified in a case like this, should he

have betrayed fear.—Henry's heart sunk within him—his knees smote together, and upon the chamber door being opened, and his name uttered in a hollow voice, he dropped the portrait to the floor; and sat, as if rivetted to the chair, without daring to lift up his eyes. At length, however, as silence again prevailed, he ventured for a moment to raise his eyes, when—my blood freezes as I relate it—before him stood the figure of Mary in a shroud—her beamless eyes fixed upon him with a vacant stare; and her bared bosom exposing a most deadly gash. " Henry!—Henry!!—Henry!!!" she repeated in a hollow tone —" Henry! I come for thee! thou hast often said that death with me was preferable to life without me; come then, and enjoy with me all the ecstacies of love these ghastly features, added to the contemplation of a charnel-house, can inspire;" then grasping his hand with her icy fingers, he swooned; and instantly found himself—stretched on the hearth of his master's kitchen; a romance in his hand, and the house dog by his side, whose cold nose touching his hand, had awaked him.

FRIENDS

It is with feelings of the deepest regret that we are at present compelled, for the support of our friends and families, to offer this simple, but true tale to your notice, trusting, at the same time, that you will be pleased to purchase this paper, it being the only means at present to support the tender thread of our existence, and keep us and our families from utter starvation which at present surrounds us.

PRICE ONE PENNY.

Printed for Author and Vendor.

264 THE HISTORY OF

MURDER OF CAPTAIN LAWSON.

CRUEL AND INHUMAN MURDER,
LAST NIGHT.

THE SCARBOROUGH TRAGEDY.

———:o:———

Giving an Account how Susan Forster, a Farmer's Daughter, near Scarborough, was seduced by Mr. Robert Sanders, a Naval Officer, under promise of Marriage.—How she became Pregnant, and the wicked hardened and cruel Wretch appointed her to meet him at a well-known, retired spot, which she unhappily did, and was basely Murdered by him, and buried under a Tree—and of the wonderful manner in which this base Murder was brought to light, and he committed to Gaol.

———:o:———

YOUNG virgins fair of beauty bright,
    And you that are of Cupid's fold,
Unto my tragedy give ear,
    For it's as true as e'er was told.

In Yorkshire, liv'd a virgin fair,
   A farmer's only daughter dear,
And a young sea-captain did her ensnare,
   Whose station was her father near.

Susannah was this maiden's name,
   The flower of all that country,
This officer a courting came,
   Begging that she his love would be.
Her youthful heart to love inclin'd
   Young Cupid bent his golden bow,
And left his fatal dart behind,
   Which prov'd Susannah's overthrow.

Ofttimes at evening she would repair,
   Close to the borders of the sea,
Her treach'rous love would meet her there,
   The time it passed most pleasantly.
And while they walked the sea-banks over,
   To mark the flowing of the tide,
He said he'd be her constant lover,
   And vow'd that she should be his bride.

   *   *   *   *   *   *

He did confess—they dug the ground while hundreds came to view,
And here the murder'd corpse they found, of her who lov'd so true;
In irons now in Prison strong lamenting he does lie;
And, by the laws condemn'd ere long, most justly he will die.

J. CATNACH, Printer, 2, Monmouth-court, 7 Dials.

HORRID MURDER,

Committed by a Young Man on a Young Woman.

———:o:———

George Caddell became acquainted with Miss Price and a degree of intimacy subsisted between them, and Miss Price, degraded as she was by the unfortunate step she had taken, still thought herself an equal match for one of Mr. Caddell's rank of life. As pregnancy was shortly the result of their intimacy, she repeatedly urged him to marry her, but he resisted her importunities for a considerable time. At length she heard of his paying addresses to Miss Dean, and threatened in case of his non-compliance, to put an end to all his prospects with that young lady, by discovering everything that had passed between them. Hereupon he formed a horrid resolution of murdering her, for he could neither bear the thought of forfeiting the esteem of a woman whom he loved, nor of marrying one who had been as condescending to another as to himself. So he called on Miss Price on a Saturday and requested her to walk with him in the fields on the following day, in order to arrange a plan for their intended marriage. Miss Price met him at the time appointed, on the road leading to Burton, at a house known by the name of the "Nag's Head." Having accompanied her supposed lover into the fields, and walked about till towards evening, they sat down under a hedge, where after a little conversation, Caddell suddenly pulled out a knife and cut her throat, and made his escape, but not before he had waited till she was dead. In the distraction of his mind he left behind him the knife with which he perpetrated the deed, and his Case of Instruments. On the following morning, Miss Price being found murdered in the field, great numbers went to take a view of her body, among whom was the woman of the house where she lodged, who recollected that she said she was going to walk with Mr. Caddell, on which the instruments were examined and sworn to have belonged to him. He was accordingly taken into custody.

J. CATNACH, Printer, Monmouth Court.

THE SECRETS REVEALED,
OR THE
FASHIONABLE LIFE OF LORD & LADY ******.

DREADFUL MURDER BY A SOLDIER,
YESTERDAY MORNING.

The Liverpool Tragedy.

Showing how a Father and Mother barbarously Murdered their own Son.

———:o:———

A few days ago a sea-faring man, who had just returned to England after an absence of thirty years in the East Indies, called at a lodging-house, in Liverpool, for sailors, and asked for supper and a bed; the landlord and landlady were elderly people, and apparently poor. The young man entered into conversation with them, invited them to partake of his cheer, asked them many questions about themselves and their family, and particularly of a son who had gone to sea when a boy, and whom they had long given over as dead. At night the landlady shewed him to his room, and when she was leaving him he put a large purse of gold into her hand, and desired her to take care of it till the morning, pressed her affectionately by the hand, and bade her good night. She returned to her husband and shewed the accursed gold: for its sake they mutually agreed to murder the traveller in his sleep.

In the dead of the night, when all was still, the old couple silently creeped into the bed room of their sleeping guest, all was quiet: the landlady approached the bedside, and then cut his throat, severed his head from his body; the old man, upwards of seventy years of age, holding the candle. They put a washing-tub under the bed to catch his blood, and then ransacking the boxes of the murdered man they found more gold, and many handsome and costly articles, the produce of the East Indies, together, with what proved afterwards, to be a marriage certificate.

In the morning early, came a handsome and elegantly dressed lady, and asked, in a joyous tone, for the traveller who arrived the night before. The old people seemed greatly confused, but said he had risen early and gone away. "Impossible!" said the lady, and bid them go to his bed-room and seek him, adding, "you will be sure to know him as he has a mole on his left arm in the shape of a strawberry. Besides, 'tis your long lost son who has just returned from the East Indies, and I am his wife, and the daughter of a rich planter long settled and very wealthy. Your son has come to make you both happy in the evening of your days, and he resolved to lodge with you one night as a stranger, that he might see you unknown, and judge of your conduct to wayfaring mariners."

The old couple went up stairs to examine the corpse, and they found the strawberry mark on its arm, and they then knew that they had murdered their own son, they were seized with horror, and each taking a loaded pistol blew out each other's brains.

———:o:———

PRINTED BY J. CATNACH.—Sold by Marshall, Bristol.

Just Published.—A Variety of Children's Books, Battledores, Lotteries, and a quantity of Popular Songs set to Music. Cards, &c., Printed cheap.

THE LIFE,
TRIAL, CHARACTER, CONFESSION, BEHAVIOUR, AND EXECUTION OF
JAMES WARD,

Aged 25, who was hung in the front of the Gaol, For the wilful Murder he committed on the Body of his own Wife.

To which is added a Copy of Affectionate Verses which he composed in the Condemned Cell The night before his
EXECUTION.

——:o:——

PRINTED AT LONDON.
PRICE ONE PENNY.

THE ARREST OF THE PRISONER.

———:o:———

"For murder, though it have no tongue, will speak with most miraculous organ."

———:o:———

The prisoner was arrested while drinking with his companions in a public-house, and after two Magistrates had heard the evidence he was fully committed to the Assizes to be tried before my Lord Judge and a British Jury, at the County Hall.

THE TRIAL!

"Whoso diggeth a pit shall fall therein."

At an early hour on the morning of the trial, the Court was crowded to excess, the Judge taking his seat at nine o'clock. The Prisoner on being placed at the bar, pleaded "Not Guilty," in a firm tone of voice. The Trial lasted many hours, when, having been found 'GUILTY.' the learned Judge addressed the prisoner as follows :—

"Prisoner, you have been found guilty of a most cold-blooded Murder, a more deliberate murder I never heard of. You and your wife had been to a neighbouring town, and were returning home, when you did it. She was found in a ditch. I cannot hold out the slightest hope of mercy towards you in this case." During this address the whole court was melted into tears. His Lordship then put on the black cap and passed the sentence as usual, holding out no hope of mercy to the prisoner.

THE COUNTY GAOL.

THE HISTORY OF

THE HOME OF THE GOOD MAN.

———:0:———

"Sundry blessings hang about his Throne, that speak him full of Grace."

———:0:———

LETTER WRITTEN BY THE PRISONER AFTER HIS CONDEMNATION.

DEAR SISTER,   Condemned Cell.

When you receive this you will see that I am condemned to die; my Father and Mother are coming to take their last farewell, and I should very much liked to have seen you, but knowing that you are on the eve of bringing into the world another to your family, I beg that you will refrain from coming; if that you do serious may be the consequences, therefore, dear Sister, do not attempt to come. I hope that no one will upbraid you for what I have done; So God bless you and yours; farewell! dear Sister, for ever.

J. WARD.

THE EXECUTION

"A threefold cord is not quickly broken."

The Execution of the above prisoner took place early this morning at eight o'clock, the people flocking to the scene at an early hour. As the period of the wretched man's departure drew near, the chaplain became anxious to obtain from him a confession of the justice of his sentence. He acknowledged the justice of his sentence, and said he was not fit to live, and that he was afraid to die, but he prayed to the Lord for forgiveness, and hoped through the merits of his Saviour that his prayer would be heard. Having received the sacrament, the executioner was not long in performing his office. The solemn procession moved towards the place of Execution, the chaplain repeating the confession words, "In the midst of life we are in death." Upon ascending the platform he appeared to tremble very much. The cap being drawn over his eyes and the signal given, the wretched man was launched into eternity. He died almost without a struggle. After the body had hanged the usual time it was cut down and buried according to the sentence in the gaol.

THE HOME OF THE BAD MAN.

———:o:———

"One Sin doth another provoke."

———:o:———

COPY OF VERSES.

Come all you feeling hearted christians, wherever you may be,
Attention give to these few lines, and listen unto me;
Its of this cruel murder, to you I will unfold,
The bare recital of the same will make your blood run cold.

Confined within a lonely cell, with sorrow I am opprest,
The very thought of what I've done, deprives me of rest;
Within this dark and gloomy cell in the County Gaol I lie,
For murder of my dear wife I am condemned to die.

For four long years I'd married been, I always lov'd her well,
Till at length I was overlooked, oh shame for me to tell;
By Satan sure I was beguiled, he led me quite astray,
Unto another I gave way on that sad unlucky day.

I well deserve my wretched fate, no one can pity me,
To think that I in cold blood could take the life away;
I took a stake out of the hedge and hit on the head,
My cruel blows I did repeat until she were dead.

I dragged the body from the stile to a ditch running by,
I quite forgot there's one above with an all-seeing eye,
Who always brings such deeds to light, as you so plainly see,
I questioned was about it and took immediately.

The body's found, the inquest held, to prison I was sent,
With shame I do confess my sin, with grief I do repent;
And when my trial did come on, I was condemned to die,
An awful death in public scorn, upon the gallows high.

While in my lonely cell I lie, the time draws on apace,
The dreadful deeds that I have done appear before my face;
While lying on my dreadful couch, those horrid visions rise,
The ghastly form of my dear wife appears before my eyes.

Oh may my end a warning be now unto all mankind,
And think of my unhappy fate and bear me in your mind;
Whether you are rich or poor, young wives and children love,
So God will fill your fleeting days with blessings from above.

THE
BURNING SHAME.
OR

MORALITY ALARMED
IN THIS NEIGHBOURHOOD.

JUST PUBLISHED
PRICE ONE PENNY.

A short time since, some of the moral-mending crew of Parsons, Magistrates, Quakers, Shakers, Puritans, Old Maids, and highly respectable, and, now retired from active business "Young Ladies," who now assume a virtue, though they have it not, and a variety of other goodly persons ever ready to compound for sins they are inclined to, by exposing those they have no mind to, living not 50 miles hence, determined on reforming doings, manners, and customs :—

IN THIS TOWN !

and a meeting in consequence took place at " Rosebud Cottage" the residence of Miss Mary Ann Lovitt, when, as a first step, it was determined to remove the facilities and *accommodation* afforded a certain— *You-know-what!* crime very general *in this neighbourhood* by hunting out of the town :—

A CERTAIN LADY ABBESS!!

who keeps a very genteel house for the *accommodation* ot "single young men and their wives" and one who never offends, or bores her patrons by asking for a sight of their 'Marriage Certificates.'

At the meeting, the armchair was taken by the Rev. John—————B.A., of this parish, Mr. Churchwarden Smith, and Mr. J. Brown, the draper, supporting him on either side; when a variety of methods were suggested for the removal of the alledged social evil, one thought *entreaty* might best answer, another was for *force*, a third recommended the Religious Tract Society, while a fourth was for the aid of the Very Rev. Rowland H———l, Miss A. and Miss B. were both loud in their praise of the Rev. Jabez B———g, mention was made of the Society for the Suppression of Vice, at length the Reverend Divine Chairman was called on for his opinion, when he—conscious of the integrity and purity of his own life and *experience*! at once pronounced :—

A BURNING SHAME!!!

as the only effectual remedy for the ever increasing evil. This was indeed a harsh measure, and some of the worthies looked a variety of colours on the occasion, but as none had the moral courage for personal character sake to oppose the parson's proposition, it was carried unanamously. A board bearing on it in legible characters :—

BEWARE OF A BAD HOUSE!!!!

was soon prepared, and with a lanthorn attached, was paraded before the house of the fair—but frail duenna's mansion. It did not remain long in this position as the following letter from the lady abbess of the *Agapemone!* soon had its deserved effect:—

GENTLEMEN:—"If the board and lanthorne is not removed from the front of my house in one hour from this time, I will publish the *name*, *profession*, and *address*, of every *gentleman*—together with that of the *lady* accompaning him who has visited my "*Establishment for Young Ladies*" during the last six months. Some of your worships know on whom this would fall heaviest."

Yours with thanks for past favours,

AUNT.

It is almost needless to say that the *board and lanthorne* were very soon removed, and, that, the old, and *accommodating* lady is doing a good business again:—

THUS CONSCIOUS DOES MAKE COWARDS OF US ALL.

THE FULL, TRUE
AND
PARTICULAR ACCOUNT
OF THE

EXTRAORDINARY MARRIAGE
That took place in THIS TOWN on Thursday last.

LONDON:
PRINTED FOR THE VENDORS.

PRICE ONE PENNY.

"Who would have thought he had been a—
He was such—a nice young man."

About a week since, a dashing young blade, dressed in the very height of the prevailing fashion, having long black and curly hair, together with a pair of out-and-out slap-up whiskers and moustaches, and calling himself Count de Coburgh Aingarpatzziwutchz, and professing to be a foreigner and a man of enormous fortune, and one of the *haut ton!* took up his lodging at the principal inn, The ——— Arms, in this town, where the swell foreigner looking blade soon made a great stir among the ladies of the place; the old, the young, the tall, the short, the fair, and the dark, were all alike smitten over head and ears in love with the distinguished visitor, but none seemed to make so much impression upon his heart as Mary Jane Jemima S———w, the youngest of the landlord's daughters of

The ———— Arms Inn, of this town. She is well known in this neighbourhood to be very handsome, with light brown hair all in ringlets, light blue eyes, a fine aquiline nose, and of a tall and commanding figure, aged about sweet **17** years of age, and very tender.

The foreign Count! soon won the affections of the young lady, and while she was all **cock-a-hoop** at the thought of having such a fine handsome young **blade** for a husband, all the other women of the town, old and young, were ready to tear out her eyes and boil them in their own blood with **womanly vexation** and revenge, and spoke of the intended **bridegroom** as the Count *Don't-know-who!*

On Thursday the bells of the old parish church rang merrily ding!-dong!!-ding!!! and the happy couple were married, our old and respected Rector officiating; assisted by his Curate, Rev. Mr. ————, and all the parish was gay from one end to the other.

A few hours after the ceremony had taken place, whilst the happy couple were feasting on all of the very best with their friends and relations, a stranger, fat and greasy, and looking like a master or journeyman butcher in his Sunday clothes, and about forty years of age, and black whiskers, made his appearance, and not being acquainted with the occasion that brought the party together, without hesitation exclaimed, loud enough to be heard by all in the room, "Well, brother-blade, you are a lucky fellow! the business about Sal Saunders is all settled to our satisfaction, the lawyer made a good job of it for you, poleaxed the lot on the other side in prime style, and skinned 'em alive, so you may now return home to Whitechapel and put on your blue apron and steel."—The company stood aghast, the bride fainted, and all was confusion. At length it came out that the newly-married man had a wife and four children at home, and that his visit to the above town was in consequence of a woman swearing a child to him. In the midst of the confusion which this discovery occasioned, the bridegroom and his brother slaughterman from Whitechapel—which is in London—made a sudden retreat, and—have not since been heard of.

THE EFFECTS OF LOVE.

SAD SHOCKING NEWS!

CRUEL SEDUCTION: DREADFUL WARNING TO ALL YOUNG WOMEN IN THIS NEIGHBOURHOOD TO BEWARE OF YOUNG MEN'S DELUDING AND FLATTERING TONGUES.

—:o:—

The following melancholy account of her cruel seduction and desertion by her base lover was forwarded to that very worthy man Mr.———a churchwarden, well-known and respected by all in this neighbourhood by Miss S——h W——r, the night before she committed suicide.

Young lovers all I pray draw near,
Sad shocking news you soon shall hear,
And when that you the same are told,
It will make your very blood run cold.

Miss S—h W—Is my name,
I brought myself to grief and shame,
By loving one that ne'er loved me,
My sorrow now I plainly see.

Mark well the words that will be said,
By W— E— I was betray'd,
By his false tongue I was beguil'd
At length to him I proved with child.

At rest with him I ne'er could be,
Until he had his will of me,
To his fond tales I did give way,
And did from paths of virtue stray.

My grief is more than I can bear,
I am disregarded every where,
Like a blooming flower I am cut down,
And on me now my love does frown.

Oh ! the false oathes he has sworn to me,
That I his lawful bride should be,
May I never prosper night, or day,
If I deceive you, he would say.

But now the day is past and gone,
That he fix'd to be married on,
He scarcely speaks when we do meet,
And strives to shun me in the street.

I did propose on Sunday night,
To walk once more with my heart's delight,
On the Umber's banks where billows roar,
We parted there to meet no more.

His word was pledged unto me,
He never shall prosper nor happy be,
The ghost of me and my infant dear,
They both shall haunt him every where.

William dear when this you see,
Remember how you slighted me,
Farewell vain world ; false man adieu,
I drown myself for love of you.

As a token that I died for love,
There will be seen a milk-white dove,
Which over my watery tomb shall fly,
And there you'll find my body lie.

These cheeks of mine once blooming red,
Must now be mingled with the dead,
From the deep waves to a bed of clay,
Where I must sleep till the Judgement Day.

A Joyful rising then I hope to have,
When Angels call me from the grave
Receive my soul, O Lord most high,
For broken hearted I must die.

Grant me one favour that's all I crave,
Eight pretty maidens let me have,
Dress'd all in white a comely show,
To carry me to the grave below.

Now all young girls I hope on earth,
Will be warned by my untimely death,
Take care sweet maidens when you are young,
Of men's deluding—flattering tongue.

PRINTED IN LONDON FOR THE VENDERS.

SHOCKING RAPE
AND
DREADFUL MURDER OF TWO LOVERS.

SHOWING HOW JOHN HODGES, A FARMER'S SON,
COMMITTED A RAPE UPON JANE WILLIAMS,
AND AFTERWARDS MURDERED HER AND
HER LOVER, WILLIAM EDWARDS,
IN A FIELD NEAR PAXTON.

———:o:———

This is a most revolting murder. It appears Jane Williams was keeping company, and was shortly to be married to William Edwards, who was in the employment of Farmer Hodges. For some time a jealousy existed in John Hodges, who made vile proposals to the young girl, who although of poor parents was strictly virtuous. The girl's father also worked on Farmer Hodges' estate. On Thursday last she was sent to the farm to obtain some things for her mother, who was ill; it was 9 o'clock in the evening when she set out, a mile from the farm. Going across the fields she was met by the farmer's son, who made vile proposals to her, which she not consenting to, he threw her down, and accomplished his vile purpose. In the meantime her lover had been to her house, and finding she was gone to the farm, went to meet her. He found her in the field crying, and John Hodges standing over her with a bill-hook, saying he would kill her if she ever told. No one can tell the feelings of the lover, William Edwards. He rushed forward, when Hodges, with the hook, cut the legs clean from his body, and with it killed the poor girl, and then run off. Her father finding she did not return, went to look for her, when the awful deeds were discovered. Edwards was still alive, but died shortly afterwards from loss of blood, after giving his testimony to the magistrates. The farmer's son was apprehended, and has been examined and committed to take his trial at the next assizes.

Thousands of persons followed the unfortunate lovers to the grave, where they were both buried together.

—: o :—

COPY OF VERSES.

—: o :—

Jane Williams had a lover true
And Edwards was his name,
Whose visits to her father's house,
Had welcome now became.

In marriage soon they would be bound,
  A loving man and wife,
But John Hodges, a farmer's son
  With jealousy was rife.

One night he met her in the fields,
  And vile proposals made:
How can I do this wicked thing,
  Young Jane then weeping said.

He quickly threw her on the ground,
  He seized her by surprise,
And did accomplish his foul act
  Despite her tears and cries.

Her lover passing by that way,
  Discovered her in tears,
And when he found what had been done
  He pulled the monster's ears.

Young Hodges with the bill-hook,
  Then cut young Edwards down;
And by one fatal blow he felled
  Jane Williams on the ground.

There side by side the lovers lay
  Weltering in their blood:
Young Jane was dead, her lover lived,
  Though ebb'd away life's flood.

Old Williams sought his daughter dear,
  When awful to relate,
He found her lifeless body there,
  Her lover's dreadful fate.

Now in one grave they both do lie,
  These lovers firm and true,
Who by a cruel man were slain
  Who'll soon receive his due.

In prison now he is confined,
  To answer for the crime.
Two lovers that he murdered,
  Cut off when in their prime.

A Funny DIALOGUE

BETWEEN A FAT BUTCHER And A  MACKEREL In Newport Market Yesterday.

BUTCHER.—Well, Mr. Mackerel, pray let me ask you how you come to show your impudent face among those who don't want to see you or any of your crew?

MACKEREL.—That my company is not agreeable to many such as you I very well know; but here I am, and will keep my place in spite of you. Don't think to frighten me with your lofty looks, Mr. Green. You are an enemy to the poor, I am their true friend, and I will be in spite of you.

BUTCHER.—I will soon see the end of you and your vain boasting, What's the poor to me?

MACKEREL.—I and thousands of my brethren are come to town for the sole good of the industrious poor. We will soon pull down your high prices, your pride and consequence, and Melt your fat off your overgrown Carcass. I am their sworn friend, and although you are biting off your tongue with vexation, yet I am determined they shall have a cheap Meal—good, sweet, and wholesome—put that in your pipe and smoke it.

BUTCHER.—Aye, aye. You are a saucy set, confound you altogether. Oddzbobs, I wish the Devil had the whole of your disagreeable tribe.

MACKEREL.—I would advise you, Mr. Green, not to show your teeth when you can't bite. Millions of my friends are on their way to town to make the poor rejoice. We have had a fine seed time, everything looks promising. Meat must and will come down. The poor will sing for joy, and you may go hang yourself in your garters.

Catnach, Printer, 2, Monmouth Court,
Cards, Bills, &c., Printed on Low Terms.

Catnach, to the day of his retirement from business in 1838, when he purchased the freehold of a disused public-house, which had been known as the Lion Inn, together with the grounds attached at Dancer's Hill, South Mimms, near Barnet, in the county of Middlesex, worked and toiled in the office of the "Catnach Press," in which he had moved as the pivot, or directing mind, for a quarter of a century. He lived and died a bachelor. His only idea of all earthly happiness and mental enjoyment was now to get away in retirement to a convenient distance from his old place of business, so to give him an opportunity occasionally to go up to town and have a chat and a friendly glass with one or two old paper-workers and ballad-writers, and a few others connected with his peculiar trade who had shown any disposition to work when work was to be done. To them he was always willing to give or advance a few pence or shillings, in money or stock, and a glass—

> "Affliction's sons are brothers in distress;
> A brother to relieve, how exquisite the bliss!"

But Jemmy knew the men that were "skulkers," as he termed them, and there was no coin, stock, or a glass for them. He invariably drank whiskey, a spirit not in general demand in England in those days. Gin was then, as now, the reigning favourite with the street folks. When the question was put to him in reference to his partiality to whiskey, he always replied—the Scotch blood proudly rising in his veins, and with a strong Northumberland burr, which never wholly forsook him, particularly when warmed by argument or drink—that, "He disdained to tipple with 'stuff,' by means of which all the women of the town got drunk. I am of Catnach. Yes! there's Catnach blood in me. Catnach—King Catnach—Catnach, King of the

Picts. We descend in a right straight line from the Picts. That's the sort of blood-of-blood that flows in the veins of all the true-bred Catnachs." Jemmy would be for continually arguing when in his cups, and the old **and the** more artful of the street-folk would let him have all the say and grandeur that he then felt within him on the subject, **well** knowing that they would be much more likely to have their glasses replenished by agreeing with him than by contradicting him. Even in his sober moments Jemmy always persisted, right or wrong, **that the Catnachs, or Catternachs, were** descended direct from a King of the Picts. Yet, **what** is somewhat anomalous, **he was** himself a rigid churchman and a staunch old Tory, "one of the olden time," and "as full of the glorious Constitution as the first volume of Blackstone."

On Catnach's retirement from the business, he left it to **Mrs. Annie Ryle**, his sister, charged, nevertheless, to the amount of £1,000 payable at his death to the estate of his niece, **Marion Martha Ryle.** In the meanwhile Mr. James Paul acted as managing man for Mrs. Ryle. This Mr. Paul—of whom Jemmy was very fond, and rumour saith, had no great dislike to the mother—had grown from a boy to a man in the office of the "**Catnach Press.**" He was therefore, well acquainted with the customers, by whom he was much respected; and it was by his tact and judgment that the business was kept so well together. He married a Miss **Crisp**, the daughter of a publican in the immediate neighbourhood.

Catnach did not long enjoy or survive **his retirement.** After the novelty of looking, as the poet Cowper puts it, and no doubt in his case found it, "Through the loop-holes of retreat, to see the stir of the Great Babel, and not feel the crowd," had worn itself out, "James Catnach, Gentleman, formerly of Monmouth Court, Monmouth Street, Printer," grew dull in his "Old Bachelor's Box;" he was troubled with hypochondriasis, and a liver overloaded with bile, and was further off than ever from being a happy man. He had managed to rake and scrape together—as far as we can get any knowledge—some £5,000 or £6,000, although £10,000 and upwards is mostly put down to him. However, he had grabbed for and caught a fair amount of "siller and gold," but it failed to realize to him—

> An elegant sufficiency, content,
> Retirement, rural quiet, friendship, books,
> Ease and alternate labour, useful life,
> Progressive virtue, and approving Heaven!

No! all he had realized was that unenviable position so popularly known as of a man not knowing what to do with himself. His visits to town were now much more frequent and of longer duration, and for hours he would sit and loiter about the shops and houses of his old neighbours, so that he might catch a glimpse, or enjoy a friendly chat with his old friends and customers. At length he got sick at heart, "wearied to the bone," and sighed for the bustle of London Life.

From the following letter written to his sister, Mrs. Ryle, in 1840, and now before us, we glean something of his state of mind and bodily health :—

July, 4th, 40.

Dear Sister,—

I have been very ill for these last three weeks. I was obliged to send for Dr. Morris to cup me, which did some good for a few days, since then the pains have gone into my breast and ribs, and for the last three days I have kept my bed, and could take nothing but a little tea and water-gruel. I wish you to procure me 6 Bills to stick on my window shutters, outside and in, "This House to be Let," and send them with ½lb Tea as soon as possible— but do not send them by Salmon's Coach, for he will not leave them at

Jackson's as Wild does, but sends a boy with it, which costs me double porterage. I feel the loss of my jelly now I am so ill, and can eat little or nothing, it would have done my throat good. I have a great crop of black and red berries [currants] if you choose I will send them up, and you can make some jelly for us both; let me know as soon as you can, say Wednesday morning and I will make the Postwoman call for the parcel at Jackson's. I also wish you to enquire of Carr what is the lowest he will take for the rooms over Mrs. Morgan, by the ½ year.

I have nothing more to say but to be remembered to Mary and Paul, and remain

Yours truly

James Catnach

Pray send a paper of the execution of the Valet, and the trial of Oxford—Mrs. Westley has not sent me 1 paper since I was last in town—neither has Thornton.

Mrs. Ryle,
    2 & 3, Monmouth Court,
        Compton Street, London.

Ultimately Catnach hired the rooms he speaks about in the body of his letter to his sister, which were on the first floor of No. 6, Monmouth Court. All the vacant space in his old premises being now fully occupied by Mrs. Ryle, and her assistants, now "the humble cottage fenc'd with osiers round," which to his leisure afforded no pleasure, was entirely deserted, and in London he fretted out the remaining portion of his life. He soon grew peevish, and his brain got a little out of balance, then he listlessly wandered in and out of the streets, courts, and alleys, "infirm of purpose." On stormy days and nights to stand and view the lightning from Waterloo Bridge was his special delight, and wonder. His temper and liver were now continually out of order, and which whiskey, even " potations pottle deep," failed to relieve. At length he died of jaundice, in the very London court in which he had muck'd and grubbed for the best part of his life, on the first day of February, 1841. Like other great men of history he has several *locales* mentioned as his final resting-place—Hornsey, Barnet, South Mimms, &c.

Urbes, certarunt septem de patria Homeri,
Nulla domus vivo patria fuit.

Seven cities strove whence Homer first should come,
When living, he no country had nor home:—*Tom Nash, 1599.*

SEVEN Grecian cities vied for Homer dead,
Through which the living Homer begged his bread.

Seven cities vied for Homer's birth, with emulation pious,—
Salamis, Samos, Colophon, Rhodes, Argos, Athens, Chios.
—*From the Greek.*

But Catnach lies buried in Highgate Cemetery, in one of the two plots that Mrs. Ryle purchased sometime previous to her brother's death. The official number of the grave is 256, SQUARE 29, over which is placed a flat stone, inscribed:—

IN MEMORY OF
JAMES CATNACH,
Of Dancer's Hill.
DIED 1st FEBRUARY, 1841,
Aged 49.

ANNE RYLE,

Sister to the above, and widow of Joseph Ryle, who died in India, 10th October, 1823. She died 20th April, 1870,
Aged 75.
Blessed are the dead which die in the Lord.

The freehold in the other plot of ground, after Catnach's death, was transferred to Mr. Robert Palmer Harding, the accountant of London, who married Catnach's niece. The stone records the death of ELIZABETH CORNELIA, third daughter of Robert Palmer Harding and Marion Martha Harding, born 9 June, 1848, died 8 of November, 1848; and GREVILLE, second son of the above, born 29 May, 1856, died 3 September, 1856. This grave is now numbered 5179. We have been thus minute in respect to Catnach's grave, from the circumstance of our having received so many contradictory statements as to its whereabouts. But however, we have removed all doubt from our mind by a personal visit to the Highgate Cemetery where under the guidance of the very civil and obliging superintendent of the grounds, Mr. W. F. Tabois, we were conducted to the spot we required, then introduced to Mr. Marks, the sexton, "here man and boy thirty years," and whom we found very intelligent and communicative on various *subjects*—

"From *grave* to gay, from lively to severe."

After Catnach's death, Mr. James Paul entered into partnership with Mrs. Ryle, and then the business was carried on under the title and style of A. Ryle and Paul. In 1845 the partnership was dissolved, Mr. Paul receiving £800 in settlement. He then entered into the public line taking the Spencer's Arms, at the corner of the Monmouth Court. A son that was born to him in 1847, he had christened James Catnach Paul. He died in the year 1870, just six weeks after Mrs. Ryle, and lies buried in the next grave but one to Catnach and his sister.

After Mr. Paul had left the business it was carried on as Ryle & Co., and ultimately became the property of Mr. W. S. Fortey, who still carries on the old business in the same quarter.

For the purpose of clearing up, if possible, some contradictory statements, a few years ago we made personal search through the musty-fusty red-tapeism of Doctor's Commons for the Will and Testament—or "Last Dying Speech" of "James Catnach, of Dancer's Hill, South Mimms, in the county of Middlesex, Gentleman, formerly of Monmouth Court, Monmouth Street, Printer," an office copy of which, together with Probate and Administration Act, we give below, by which it will be seen that the Personal Effects are sworn to as under three hundred pounds. But this gives us no idea of the value of his "Freehold, Copyhold, or Leasehold Estate" mentioned in the body of the Will.

"Extracted from the principal Registry of Her Majesty's Court of Probate.

"In the Prerogative Court of Canterbury—

"**This is the last Will and Testament** of me JAMES CATNACH of Dancers Hill, South Mimms in the County of Middlesex Gentleman formerly of Monmouth Court Monmouth Street Printer I direct that my just debts funeral and testamentary expences be paid as soon as conveniently may be after my decease and subject thereto I give devise and bequeath all **my real and** personal Estate whatever and wheresoever and of what nature or kind soever to my Sister Anne the Widow of Joseph Ryle now residing in Monmouth Court aforesaid her heirs executors and administrators according to the nature and qualities thereof respectively In trust nevertheless for her Daughter Marion Martha Ryle her heirs executors administrators and assigns respectively when she shall attain the age of twenty one years absolutely with power in the meantime to apply the rents interest dividends or proceeds thereof for and towards the maintenance education and advancement of the said Marion Martha Ryle and notwithstanding the private means of my said Sister may be adequate to such purpose but if the said Marion Martha Ryle shall depart this life before she shall attain the age of twenty one years then I give devise and bequeath all my said real and personal Estate to my said Sister her heirs executors administrators and assigns absolutely I hereby direct that during the minority of the said Marion Martha Ryle it shall be lawful for the said Anne Ryle her heirs executors administrators to demise or lease all or any part of my freehold copyhold or leasehold Estate for any term consistent with the tenure thereof not exceeding twenty one years so that on every such demise the best yearly rent be reserved that can be obtained for the property which shall be therein comprised without taking any fine or premium and so that the tenant or lessee be not made dispunishable for waste I hereby nominate constitute and appoint my said Sister sole Executrix of this my Will and hereby revoking all former and other Wills by me at any time heretofore made I declare this to be my last Will and Testament In witness whereof I have hereunto set my hand the twenty second day of January one thousand eight hundred and thirty nine— JAMES CATNACH—Signed and acknowledged by the above named James Catnach as and for his last Will and Testament in the presence of us present at the same time who in his presence and the presence of each other have hereunto set our names as Witnesses—William Kinsey 13 Suffolk St. Pall Mall Solr.—Wm. Tookey his Clerk."

[The Probate and Administration Act.]

"Extracted from the principal Registry of Her Majesty's Court of Probate.

"In the Prerogative Court of Canterbury—

April, 1842.

"JAMES CATNACH — On the second day of April administration (with the Will annexed) of the Goods Chattels and Credits of James Catnach formerly of Monmouth Court Monmouth Street Printer but late of Dancers Hill South Mimms both in the county of Middlesex Gentleman deceased was granted to William Kinsey Esquire the Curator or Guardian lawfully assigned to Marion Martha Ryle Spinster a Minor the Niece and usufructuary Universal Legate until she shall attain the age of twenty one years and the absolute Universal Legatee on attaining that age named in the said Will for the use and benefit of the said minor and until she shall attain the age of twenty one years have been first sworn duly to administer Anne Ryle Widow the Sister sole Executrix Universal Legatee In trust and the contingent universal Legatee named in the said Will and also the natural and lawful Mother and next of kin of the said minor having first renounced the probate and execution of the said Will and the Letters of administration (with the said Will annexed) of the goods of the said deceased and also the Curation or Guardianship of the said Minor and consented (as by Acts of Court appear)—

EFFECTS UNDER THREE HUNDRED POUNDS.

It is gratifying to be able to record that what the late Mr. Catnach was to the masses in the way of news provider some fifty years ago, the penny papers are now, with this exception, that the former tended to lower and degrade their pursuit after knowledge, the latter, on the contrary, improve and elevate them while they amuse and instruct all who peruse their contents. With the march of intellect, and the thirst for knowledge blended with the desire for truth, out went, to a great extent, the penny broad-sheet. Several persons made the attempt to revive it long after the death of the great original Jemmy Catnach, but without success.

—:o:—

☞ The be-all and the end-all here.

—:o:—

INDEX.

	Page.
Adelaide, Queen	89
A Funny Dialogue	294
Alnwick—The Borough of	1
,, St. Michael's Church	2
,, Parish Register	2
,, Catnach's shop in	3
,, Register of Death	3
,, Printing Press in	4
,, The Catnach Press	4
,, The Castle	6
,, The Abbey	6
,, Davison's business	9
,, Election at	74
Attack on William IV.	88
Ballads:—Banks of the Nile	239
,, Crazy Jane	240
,, Death of Nelson	236
,, Drink to me eyes	228
,, Gallant Sailor	224
,, Meet me Willow Glen	227
,, Mistletoe Bough	229
,, Mountain Maid	226
,, O Rare Turpin	225
,, Rose will cease to blow	230
,, Scarlet Flower	237
,, Sun that lights Roses	233
,, The Thorn	238
,, True Hearted Sailor	231
,, When Bibo though fit	232
,, Woodpecker, The	234
,, Ye Topers all	235
Benton, Mrs. *nee* Elizabeth Catnach	38
Bewick, T., wood-engraver	14
Bewick Collector, The	16
Bewick :—See Books	
Bewicks Illustrations—See Books.	
Bishop and Williams	84
Black Sal and Dusty Bob	45
Books printed by John Catnach:—	
,, Beauties of Natural History	4
,, Chevy Chase	34
,, Cock Robin	8

	Page.
Books printed by John Catnach:—	
,, Dr. Johnson's Works	34
,, Hermit of Warkworth	5
,, Life of Thompson	34
,, Stockdale's Poems	4
——By Catnach and Davison :—	
,, Beattie's Minstrel	9
,, Blair's Grave	9
,, Burn's Poems	13
,, Gray's Elegy	9
——By Davison :—	
,, Crazy Jane	12
,, Ferguson's Poems	14
,, Guess Book, The	17, 32
,, Halfpenny Books	16
,, Northumberland Minstrel	15
,, Repository, The	11
——Illustrated by Bewick.	
,, Beauties of Natural History	4
,, Burn's Poems	13
,, Blair's Grave	9
,, Hermit of Warkworth	5
,, Respository, The	11
,, Stockdale's Poems	4
Brown, Mrs., murdered	91
Brunswick Theatre, The	77
Burkers, The	84
Burnie, Sir Richard	43
Burradon Ghost, The	4
Caroline, Queen, The trial of	46
Verses on	47, 48, 50
Death of	49, 51
Cato Street Conspiracy, The	45, 46
Catchpennies :—Apparitin, The	261
,, Burning Shame	281
,, Cruel Murder	264
,, Execution of Ward	273
,, Extraordinary Marriage	285
,, Horrid Murder	267
,, Liverpool Tragedy	270
,, Murder by a Soldier	269
,, Murder of Capt. Lawson	264
,, Murder of Two Lovers	291

INDEX.

	Page
Catchpennies :—	
" Secrets Revealed	269
" Scarborough Tragedy	265
" Shocking News	289
" Shocking Rape	291
Catnach, John—the father, born	1
" Married	2
" At Alnwick	3, 4, 5, 8
" At Newcastle	33
" A Bankrupt	35
" In London	35, 36
" Death of	37
Catnach, James, born 1792	2
" His early life	38
" Arrives in London	40
" Imprisoned for 6 months	43
" Queen Caroline	47
" Verses on Caroline	48
" Life in London	57, 63
" At Alnwick	75, 76
" And Mother Cummins	81
" His education	94
" Nursery books	94
" Christmas Carols	242
" His Woodcuts	257
" Dying Speeches	258
" His Retirement	295
" At Dancer's Hill	296
" Letter to his sister	297
" Return to London	298
" Death of	299
" Will of the	301
Charlotte, The Princess of	42
" " " Death of	43
Christmas Carols	241 to 255
Collins, Dennis	88
Copy of Affectionate Verses	65, 66, 67, 68, 80, 292
Clennell, Luke	4
Corder, Wm., The murderer	79
" " Execution of	80
Cruikshank, George	54
Cruikshank, Robert	55
Cubitt's Treadmill	64
Cummins "Mother"	81
and Catnach	81-2-3
Davison of Alnwick :—	

	Page
Davison and Catnach	1
" Partnership	9-11
" His chemistry	9
" Death of	15
Dennis Collins	88
Earl Grey	87
Executions- Public of :—	
Bishop and Williams	85
Courvoisier	92
Corder	92
Fauntleroy, Mr. H., banker	73
Five Pirates, The	92
Greenacre	92
Muller	92
Mannings	92
Pegsworth	91
Thurtell	72
False News, circulating of	14
Flying Stationer, The	66
Fortey, Mr	242-300
George the III, death of	45
George the IV	45
Goldie, Mr., of Alnwick	94
Graham, printer, Alnwick	39
Greenacre and Gale	91
Gurney, Mr. Baron	89
Haines, Mrs. née Mary Catnach	38
" Hanging Matches "	65
Hugo, Rev. Thomas	13, 15
" his Bewick collector	16, 39
Jane Williams	292
Juvenile Books :—	
A Apple Pie	177
Butterfly's Ball	163
Cinderella	203
Cock Robin	199
Easter Gift, The	171
Golden Pippin, The	113
Good Child's Alphabet	207
Guess Book, The	17
Jack Jingle	197
Jerry Diddle	129
Jumping Joan	145

	Page.
Juvenile Books:—	
Mother Hubbard	187
New Year's Gift	205
Nurse Love-child's	97
Nursery Rhymes	193
Red Riding Hood	201
Simple Simon	195
Kent, Duke of, his death	45
Life in London, by Pierce Egan	52
" on the Stage	54
" Catnach's version 57,	63
" Thackeray on	64
Likeness of the Murderer	69
" " William Corder	79
Lindsay, Printer, &c.	4
Long, Song Seller, The	221
Marten, Maria, Murder of	78
" " Verses on	80
Mayhew's "London Labour" 69,	92
Morgan, John, Poet! ... 43, 47,	82
Paul, Mr.	296, 300
Pitts, John	40
" Old Mother	41
Pizzey, Sausage Maker, The 43,	44
Pocock, Mr. C. J. of Brighton	57
Red Barn, The	78
Reform Bill, The	87

	Page.
Ryle, Mrs. Anne	296, 297
" death of	299
" Marion Martha	296
Sarah Gale	91
Seven Dials, The Bards of	40, 41
" " The Trade in	42
" " and Queen Caroline	47
Shocking Rape and Murder	291
Smith, Mark, of Alnwick:—	
" Apprenticed to Catnach	9
" in London	35
" in Alnwick	74
" his autograph	39
" the death of	74
Songs, 3 yards-a-penny	222
Thistlewood, The Conspirator	46
Thompson, John, Life of	34
Thurtell, and Weare	70
" Execution of	72
Tom and Jerry	53, 55
" the Tears of	55
Treadmill, The	64
Vestris, Madame	89
Vint, John, Printer, &c.	4
Walker, Mr., Paternoster Row	35
Weare, Mr., Murder of	70
William the IV.	88
Willoughby family Alnwick	36

www.ingramcontent.com/pod-product-compliance
Lightning Source LLC
Chambersburg PA
CBHW030305240426
43673CB00040B/1062